FREE FROM CAPTIVITY

Biblical Secrets To Overcoming Addiction

ERIKA GREY

Pe Danté Press
Danbury, CT

Copyright © 2013 ERIKA GREY

All rights reserved. No part of this publication may be reproduced in any form without written permission from Pedante Press.

Pedante Press
Suite #4 White Oak
Danbury, CT 06810

All Scriptural quotations in this publication are from the New King James Version of the Bible © by Thomas Nelson, Inc.

Printed in the United States of America

ISBN: **097901994X**
ISBN-13: **978-0979019944**

LCCN: 2012919002

DEDICATION

I dedicate this book to Paul: without you, I would have never been able to write any of my books, including this one, which is a memorial to you my darling, who is now a casualty in this war.

For More Books by Erika Grey Go To
www.erikagrey.com
Listen to "The Erika Grey Prophecy Talk Show" on blogtalkradio

See also Erika Grey's articles, blogs and videos on her YouTube channel

Follow Erika Grey on Twitter & Facebook

CONTENTS

	Introduction	iii
1	The Anatomy of An Addict	1
2	Addictive and Mind-Altering Drugs	19
3	The Getting High Illusion	39
4	The Prison House	71
5	Freedom From The Prison	91
6	Exodus From House of Bondage	103
7	The Enemies in The Land	119
8	More	135
9	Herbs To Aid Recovery	151
10	It's Your Choice	169
	Bibliography	182

ERIKA GREY

FREE FROM CAPTIVITY

INTRODUCTION

I am a Bible prophecy writer and teacher. Those of us who follow Bible prophecy believe that we are in the End Times. The Bible tells us that in the last days perilous times will come. Men will be lovers of themselves, and sin will abound. Sin will cause all kinds of social problems. My mission as a prophecy writer is to show people how Bible prophecy lines up with current events. It is also to provide information to help those dealing with difficult life issues, which arise from living in these last days.

Jesus explains that because sin abounds the love of many will grow cold. That if he returns any later there will be no faith left on the Earth. 2 Timothy tells us that men will be lovers of themselves, proud, boastful, and brutal, without heart. Children will be disobedient to their parents. Society will be out of control. 2 Timothy describes people given over to the god of self. They become brutal, given to pleasure with no regard for their children, coworkers, parents or anyone.

Addiction is a symptom of the perilous times Timothy describes. Addiction has reached epidemic proportions. Individuals are addicted to drugs, alcohol, and all kinds of vices. Addiction is also on the rise because people are facing horrific life circumstances that can lead one into addiction. People are now dealing with unimaginably painful situations. The addict then turns around and causes grief to the family members who love him or her.

We have witnessed the breakdown of our society. The American divorce rate is 50%. In Russia it is 65% and in Belarus, the divorce rate is 68%, which means more than two-thirds of marriages in that society end up in divorce. Another 7% and the rate will be three-quarters of all marriages ending in divorce. Divorce greatly affects children. Many of the children of divorce will face abandonment issues, which cause anger, rage, and inner wounds so great that they lend to all kinds of emotional and behavioral disorders. Their pain also leads them to alcohol and drug abuse among other addictions. The list is endless of persons suffering from trauma, family violence, and sexual abuse to those who purely love pleasure who end up in the addiction spiral.

In the book of Jeremiah, God forecasts the Babylonian captivity in retribution for Israel's many sins and idolatry. Jeremiah specifically condemns the parents who burned their children in the fire to the god of Molech. The Israelites sacrificed and murdered their children to their gods. While we read this in horror and wonder how anyone can sacrifice their children for a belief in a god, many addicts abandon their children to the god of their substance.

According to the March 5, 2010 issue of the Guardian, Mark Tran's article, "Girl starved to death while parents raised virtual child in online game," recounts the story of a South Korean couple who let their three-month-old daughter starve to death while they ran off to internet cafes to play their computer games. He also retold the account of a 22-year-old male who killed his mother because she nagged him for spending too much time on the computer playing games. After killing her, he resumed playing his game.

I learned about female drug addicts who give their children as collateral to drug dealers who front them drugs. Even worse in some countries parents sell their children into slavery to buy drugs. Some of these children end up as sex slaves. While these cases are the extreme, addicts abandon or emotionally abandon their children while abusing alcohol, drugs or indulging in another addiction.

After about two-and-a-half years of sobriety, I found many emotions seeming to come to the surface. The greatest of these was anxiety. After trying the medical route of taking an SSRI (Serotonin-Specific Reuptake Inhibitor--used to treat depression) and a mild tranquilizer, I terminated all medicines and started on the path of natural and herbal medicine. For many years now, I have not taken any conventional drugs or medicine unless undergoing surgery.

FREE FROM CAPTIVITY

    I used herbal medicine and ate a healthy diet to reverse the damage from my earlier years of abuse and cigarette smoking. I succeeded in reversing the ailments my addictions caused, such as bronchitis, asthma, allergies, low blood sugar, chronic fatigue, and insomnia. Since I quit smoking, I have been through a myriad of unbelievably stressful situations and have not gone back to abuse any substances. I discovered herbal teas that are very effective for stress. While I have maintained over 26 years of sobriety from alcohol and drugs, I have battled with an addictive personality and other addictions. I have gotten the victory from each of these through the teachings in God's Word.

    The monster of alcohol and drug addiction reared its ugly head within my family. While I maintained sobriety, my husband fell off the wagon, which led to the breakup of our family. Our son also fell into the addiction prison. The effects were like an emotional tsunami that took a toll on each family member and shipwrecked the users. Dealing with a family of addicts wreaked such havoc that I found myself under considerable amounts of stress and grief. When alcoholism and drug abuse divided us and took my spouse from me, I could not let go while in the throes of my own relationship addiction. God's Word transformed me. Meanwhile, I discovered Kava root powder and started to use it on a regular basis. As life's circumstances overwhelmed me, a simple herb helped me through the difficult time of grief, loss, and stress in addition to my faith.

    It was at this time I was inspired to write this book, and use my secrets to help others who were suffering from addiction. As I struggled through the problems caused by dealing with a family of addicts, I realized that what I was experiencing was what I was writing and warning others would happen in these last days. It was now happening to my life. I phoned a preacher friend of mine about all that I was battling. He said to me that God wanted me to experience what I write about for other people. With the addiction issue again at the forefront of my life, it placed me facing 2 Timothy head on. 2 Timothy states that in the last days men are lovers of pleasure more than of God. All addicts are lovers of pleasure.

It is my hope that this book will help those who suffer from addiction to get free from their bondage, and that it will give them an approach to help maintain their sobriety from dangerous, addictive substances and vises. My desire is for hardcore addicts to find the freedom that the Bible speaks of from its prison.

This book begins by looking at the anatomy of an addict; every addict will relate to their anatomy. The addicted person is like a stick of dynamite with a fuse. Alcohol and drugs light the fuse. After helping the addict to understand him or herself, we will look at alcohol and drugs and their use worldwide. While I cover dangerous substances, I also mention other addictions such as sex, food, relationship, the internet, gambling, pornography, and work, because addicts cross over into these areas and become addicted to them.

There are insights in this book not found in any other work on addiction. *Free From Captivity* provides extensive biblical lessons on addiction along with a directory of herbs effective in helping to overcome various dependencies and heal from them.

It is my hope that this book will act as an aid for addicts and for those whose loved ones are in the throes of addiction. This is no doubt a serious issue of our times and a symptom of living in these last days.

1

THE ANATOMY OF AN ADDICT

Addicts come from all occupations. They come from all races, creeds and colors. They are rich, poor, educated and uneducated. They live all over the world. Some live in huts, other in trailers, some in houses and others; mansions. Although addicts come from diverse backgrounds, they all share the same anatomy and traits. Addicts contrast from non-addicts because their anatomies differ.

Among the parts of an addict's anatomy is a pleasure button. They also possess intense emotions and an inner void to a bottomless pit. Addicts have a heightened fright/flight response to stress and a need to escape. Additionally, a part of their makeup is their obsessive-compulsive thinking and a need to control. Addicts also share anxiety or depression and denial. They rationalize, minimize and blame others. No addict's anatomy is complete without their need to make excuses; any excuse is a reason to partake in their pleasure. Finally, all vice dependent persons have a bottom. Their body chemistry works similar to a stick of dynamite with a fuse, which lights when they partake in dangerous substances. All addicts while partaking in their obsessive pastime are prisoners and idolaters. They die to themselves for the god of their vice. Once they do this, their loved ones no longer know them because their whole personality changes. From this point forward, they live and die for their addiction, substance of choice, i.e. idol.

The Pleasure Button

As humans, we like what makes us feel good, we live for pleasure. We like those things that give us satisfaction. Our lives are often a balance of work and pleasure. For an addict, it is as if the brain short circuits during the gratification process. When something feels good, an addict wants more and attempts to keep the enjoyment center going full throttle. The addict has a pleasure button, and once the button gets pushed, the addict keeps their hand on it.

There is a giant list of addictions from food, coffee, cigarettes, alcohol, drugs, sex, work, love addiction, relationships, shopping, gambling, sports, pornography, exercise, television, the internet, movies, games, video games; the list includes anything that gives one pleasure. If chocolate gives a food addict enjoyment, he or she will finish the box. If it is work, the person will not stop working. Some addictions like work, hobbies and sports can yield positive benefits while others destroy the addict's life.

An addict is someone who cannot stop pushing the button. They will keep attempting to stimulate the pleasure center in his or her brain. They want to live for their gratification, which is an escape for them. An addict is a lover of pleasure. They live and die for their indulgences and give themselves completely over to them.

The most destructive addictions are those involving tobacco, alcohol, and drugs. These actually change brain chemistry and keep the addict dependent on the substances for pleasure and comfort. Research is finding that even non-substance addictions change brain chemistry. There is also the finding that the brains of addict's functions differently. This proves that the addict possesses a pleasure button that these studies suggest.

FREE FROM CAPTIVITY

Intense Emotions

For addicts, the overstimulation of their pleasure center acts as an escape from an inner pain that is so great, intense and overwhelming that they look to self-medicate to flee from these emotions. Many addicts suffer from mood disorder and there is a link for bipolar illness and substance abuse. Doctors theorize that those who suffer from bi-polar personality disorder abuse substances to help themselves self-medicate. This almost makes no sense. They say that an individual suffering from bi-polar mental illness will use alcohol to bring them down from a manic high. They use cocaine to lift them from their depression. Cocaine also causes severe depression and makes a non-manic person seem manic along with alcohol. The bi-polar person uses alcohol and drugs to escape their emotions or problems versus treat their disorder.

Addicts under the influence of alcohol or any drugs mimic full scale off-the-chart's mental illness. While intoxicated my alcoholic son came in my room telling me that he was bleeding out of every orifice of his body and bleeding to death. On another occasion, he told me that he could not tell the difference between his dreams and reality. On another, he insisted that he could tell the future and make me a lot of money from his dreams. . As he uttered these words with straggly unkempt hair, he sounded completely insane. When he is drunk, his facial features totally change, which added to his crazed demeanor.

On another occasion, my son became angry at a mess left by his sister in the kitchen. When we arrived home, we found the kitchen trashed, a display of cut up apples neatly arranged in a bowl with spaghetti and pasta sauce, and blood dripped everywhere. Spattered and mottled blood covered the bathroom sink, a message written in blood decorated the mirror, and blood drips speckled some stairs up to my daughter's bedroom. In her room, oatmeal covered her wall, curtains and her belongings were scattered on the floor.

I phoned my son's father to inform him about the horror scene, and he answered the phone drunk. He proceeds to phone the police for me, only he told them that I cut both kids. As the police arrived and informed me of his call, he insisted I put the police on the phone so that he can let them know we agree. At this point, I knew he was intoxicated and using this episode to retaliate against me for some, alcoholic resentment, so I would not hand the phone to them.

Speaking of my significant other, one night as he drank alcohol and smoked crack, a friend of his told me he stood up all night yelling at a wall in his kitchen. He yelled at God for making Satan and told God that He should have made him Satan because he would have at least done some good for this world. His friend told me that by morning he stood crying his eyes out and was an absolute wreck because God made Satan. The day I discovered his crack use, I walked into his mother's beach house. Heavy blankets covered each window and hung from hammered nails. This is a classic example of the insanity and paranoia that comes with crack use. I later learned that blanketed windows signal crack paranoia. My son's father, hiding his drug use, claimed his friend nailed the blankets to his mother's windows.

These are classic examples of the insanity that comes with alcohol and drug use. Therefore, the idea that a bi-polar person self-medicates is unrealistic in light of the fact that alcohol and drugs sends one's mental health off the charts of sanity. Whether one is bi-polar or not, if they are an addict, they experience intense emotions and a need to escape from the pain. An addict looks for pleasure. If they feel decent, they feel great and when they feel bad, they feel really awful. When they are in distress, they want to feel good again, it is that simple. They want bliss. For some, these intense feelings exhibit mood disorder and for others it is in fact because their lives have been difficult and traumatic. These intense, painful feelings are very hard for the addict to deal with. Addicts are born sensitive due to their body chemistry and personality.

An addict's indulgence adds to their pain as their addiction leads to the destruction of their lives through a myriad of avenues from personal relationships to arrests, accident, illness, and substance induced poverty. When they are using they spend their money on alcohol and or drugs. They feel so physically and emotionally bad afterwards because it takes such a toll on their body that they cannot make it to work or appointments. All of these dilemmas cause great stress, along with their inability to fend off the stress as the substances they abuse tears their nervous systems apart.

Inner Void or Bottomless Pit

All humans possess an inner void, but an addict's inner void goes into the depths of the abyss. It is as if they walk around with gaping holes and festering soul wounds. Their addiction is an attempt to fill a void within their souls by comforting themselves through indulging in their addiction. There is the theory that the propensity to addictions enters after traumatic experiences, which leave one feeling damaged, unloved, and rejected as a viable human being. The addiction fills the gap, but never replaces what was lost and cannot even come close to repairing it. In most instances, the addiction makes the pain worse because it is a cheap substitute and further erodes and complicates one's life. The addict often feels lower self-esteem and terrible after engaging in his or her shameful vice.

All traumas break one's spirit. Not all who have experienced trauma become addicts. Trauma is a common thread in addiction. Those who overcome disturbing events unscathed are rare. There are many different sources of trauma. Living through natural disasters, war, crime, accidents, domestic violence, physical and sexual abuse, and family discord all cause trauma. Traumas not only break one's spirit but leave one with the belief that the world is not a safe place. Painful experiences that involve victimization also leave one feeling unloved, rejected, abandoned, and worthless, which intensifies their inner void. Their innermost feelings border on terror and emptiness that is out of the abyss of Hell itself.

Rejection and abandonment leave an addict feeling such abysmal loneliness that they experience their primal fears and re-live them in their relationships. Abandonment also leaves many with rage they direct against themselves via self-destructive behavior or against others. Physical and sexual abuse, rape, crime, and torture leave its victims with feelings of worthlessness. As if they are human refuse, they re-live the trauma in their actions and seek to escape the inner void that forever haunts them through addictive behavior. They keep their hand on their pleasure button to feel the enjoyment from their vices to counter this inner void and gaping hole within them.

Heightened Flight Fright Response to Stress and Need to Escape

There is an old saying that when the going gets tough, the tough get going. For an addict when life gets difficult, the addict looks to run away from the problem. Addicts do not do well with stress, due to their intense emotions. When the stress is too great, the addict looks to flee into any escapes that will free their mind. A food addict will veer off into the pleasure of eating comfort foods. Sex addicts will initiate a sex act to take all of their focus off their problems and give themselves a mental break. The workaholic will do the same with their work because work is the place they find solace. A substance abuser will use alcohol or drugs. Whatever the addiction, all addicts possess the desire to escape from painful situations.

The action an addict takes to get to their escape comes across as high-risk behavior. When making a getaway one takes risks. If you are fleeing a fire, you run as fast as you can to safety. For an addict, escaping is about self-preservation. Taking risks goes along with escaping. When the occupants of the Twin Towers were racing down the stairs to escape the fire, they ran fast down those stairs despite the risk of falling. Some jumped out of the windows to their death to flee the fire. For an addict, the need to escape is part of their anatomy and is mistaken for high-risk behavior. Indulging in their vice is their flight and fright response and how they escape the stressors in their lives.

Food addiction, though not as high risk as other addictions, provides an escape through the pleasure from eating food and the satisfaction it provides. Comfort foods bring food addicts to a place of safety they first experienced as young children. They recall eating those foods and feeling happy, satisfied, and comforted by them. These foods were fed to them by a mother who nurtured and took care of them. Eating these foods takes food addicts back to this place of safety lodged in their earliest memories. In addition, high-carbohydrate foods cause one to release endorphins, which are nature's feel good chemicals.

Obsessive-Compulsive Thinking

When an addict is upset or even happy, the thoughts play repeatedly in their mind. If someone wrongs them, they can spend all day thinking over the details of what the person did to them. If they suffer a breakup, they become obsessive about their partner. When life is going good for them, they obsess on their success and feel a high from their feelings. If they are excited about a new project or going on a trip, this too can occupy all of their thoughts.

An addict's mind races. These thoughts enter the mind one after another and center on the same subject over and over. While obsessive thinking is a detriment, if an addict continuously focuses on a productive project, they can achieve some notable accomplishments. What is an addict's weakness is also their strength.

Obsessiveness crosses over into compulsion, which the dictionary defines as "an irresistible urge to behave in a certain way, especially against one's conscious wishes." Addiction also becomes a compulsion, and an addict lives for his or her vice and constantly tries to obtain his or her drug of choice. Compulsive behavior such as counting forks, eliminating dust, even to obsessing on how someone wronged you, along with addiction itself, provides escape from inner pain.

If the addict is under the influence or on what AA refers to as a dry drunk (meaning that their thinking is obsessive compulsive and their behavior reactive, while not using any substance) they live in a perpetual state of escaping inner pain.

Need to Control

Addicts are generally controlling individuals. They feel the need to be in control and have rule of their lives and relationships at all times. Along with this need to control, addicts perform ably with a good deal of structure because structure is safe and gives them a sense of being in control. Addicts do not do well with surprises or change.

The need to control makes an addict feel secure. Feeling in control acts as ointment for the pain from their void. Any upset to this control brings on the intense feelings felt by their emptiness, which then launches their obsessive thinking. An addict ruminates over their problem as a way to rule their situation. The obsession and need to control is a way to keep their emotionally fragile lives in equilibrium as life's circumstances threaten that balance.

Eating disorders are also another form of addiction, control, and escape. Control sprouts from fear, which springs from the inner wound. The wounded child becomes fearful of what wounded them in the first place and acts controlling as a mean to keep it from happening again. They also want to hold onto what they feel they do not have such as the love of the family member or spouse because an addict feels unworthy of anyone's love, deep down.

Anxiety and or Depression

Addicts generally are depressed and can suffer from anxiety. It is usually one or both. The anxiety and depression go back to the inner void and is part of their intense emotions that lead them to want to escape. The anxiety results from the trauma and fear suffered during their lives. If an addict has experienced trauma, they most likely suffer from post-traumatic stress disorder. PTSD and anxiety go hand in hand. Addicts will self-medicate to ease their anxiety. They will drink or drug to feel less anxious about a situation that fills them with dread.

Denial Rationalize and Minimize

Addicts deny they have a problem and will lie about their dependence to themselves and others to protect their addictive behavior. Tell an overeater that they eat too much, and they will inform you that they gain weight because of a thyroid problem. Some will state that they gain weight by looking at food. Inform a workaholic that they work too much and they will let you know how demanding their job is. A sex addict will claim that they are someone who just enjoys sex and has a high sex drive.

Addicts will even convey that they really do not partake in their pleasure that often as every one might think. Substance abusers will go the extremes of being ridiculous to convince you that they do not indulge. Such as having a beer in their hand and telling you it not a beer they are holding. In the throes of their habit they deny they have a problem to protect themselves. They will compare themselves to extreme cases as the standard to justify their use. They will rationalize and minimize in their own mind and to others.

I commented to my alcoholic family member about his having a beer at eight in the morning he replied, "There wasn't any coffee, so I thought I would have a beer." I proceeded to discuss his morning till night each day drinking pattern, and he minimalized his drinking by telling me that he really did not drink all that often. He communicated that he can control his alcohol intake, and stop after one or two drinks. For this reason, he did not have a drinking problem.

Blame Others

As part of their denial, addicts do not take responsibility for their actions but blame those around them for their use of substance or vice. In this way, they justify their actions. This behavior goes right back to Adam and Eve in the Garden of Eden when they partook of the forbidden fruit, which Adam wanted to keep eating. He blamed both God and his wife by saying, *"The woman whom you gave me to be with gave it to me, and I ate it."* The woman blamed the serpent and said that the serpent deceived her and she ate it. God then judged all of them: Adam, Eve and the Serpent. He held each of them accountable for their actions. Aaron conveyed the same response when he made the golden calf. He essentially told Moses that he did not do anything, he just threw the gold into the fire, and the calf came out of it.

Alcoholics and addicts are notorious for blaming everyone in their lives for their drinking and drugging. It is "poor me, poor me, pour me another drink." Most likely, the alcoholic and addict has family and relationship problems because of his or her drinking and or drug abuse. All addicts blame those who cause them unhappiness or grief as the cause for their indulgence in alcohol, drugs, food, sex, the internet, etc.

Any Excuse is an Excuse

While an addict likes to blame their circumstances and the people around them for their unhappiness, any excuse is an excuse to partake in their addiction. Whether they feel good, bad, happy or sad, when they celebrate or commiserate; it does not matter--whatever the problem, whatever the occasion; it is always a valid reason to indulge in their vice.

Alcoholics, drug addicts, and cigarette smokers especially make excuses for their need for their habit. Smokers going through difficult times will tell you that they cannot give them up because of the problems they are experiencing. I heard reason after reason why my son drank after he said he was going to quit. Sometimes non-addicts make excuses for the addict, by saying that they drink because of a tragedy, or can't quit smoking because there is too much stress in the person's life. Cigarette quitting excuses are the most widely accepted. Since I quit smoking cigarettes, I have experienced extremely difficult and stressful times, and have not picked up a cigarette. There is no excuse.

The addict believes that their excuse justifies their use. Their addiction of choice is now their crutch to get through life. For substance abuse, the excuses are evident. For sex, relationship, pornography, work, gambling and food addictions, the defenses are not so obvious. In the end, stress and duress set off these vices as well.

All Addicts are Like a Stick of Dynamite and Have a Fuse

Addicts are like a stick of dynamite with a fuse. Certain substances have the power to light that fuse and destroy the addict. Think of a stick of dynamite when it blows up. This is exactly what happens to an addict's life when he or she uses alcohol or drugs; their life goes up in smoke. As an addict you need to be aware that this is part of your anatomy and make sure you never light your fuse. We will address these substances in the next chapter.

All Addicts Have a Bottom

All addicts have a bottom. This is the place in the darkest recesses of the addiction prison. It lies the mud and mire of the mess the addict has made of his or her life. It is the place from where many addicts decide to get help.

There are high bottoms and low bottoms. A high bottom means that the addict did not descend as far downward as the low bottom drunk. For some, they recognize their need for help before losing everything. For others, it takes losing everything and maybe ending up in prison or maimed for the person to recognize that they need help. For some addicts there seems to be no bottom.

We hear of no bottom addicts all the time. These persons die from their use. Such as the career cocaine addict who dies of a cocaine-induced heart attack or the alcoholic who dies in an accident or who takes a dangerous combination of booze and pills. It is not that these persons did not have a bottom. They possess one like all addicts. For these addicts, death was their bottom, and it can happen early in their usage.

Addicts Do Not Pop Out of a Box

Addicts do not pop out of a box meaning that they are not exactly the same. The Manual of Mental Disorders, Third Edition, Revised (DSM-III-R) or the Diagnostic and Statistical Manual of Mental Disorders, Fourth Edition (DSM-IV) and ICD-10; classify addicts as having addictive personality disorder and group various substance abuse disorders. They state that many who suffer from bi-polar personality disorder abuse drugs to help themselves self-medicate. As I stated earlier this makes no sense because alcohol and cocaine make an addict more depressed. Cocaine drops the mood of an addict so deep into depression that they become off the charts manic.

There is also antisocial personality disorder that aligns with addictive personality disorder. It exhibits chronic lying, drinking, drug taking, and criminal behavior. Not all addicts are criminals. Some will say that all addicts lie about everything while in general, addicts lie to cover up their habit to those who might want to take it away. A person who lies about everything lies because they are a liar. To say all addicts lie about everything is putting an addict in a box.

Experts state that people with addictive personalities are sensitive to stress. They have trouble handling situations that they deem frustrating, even if the event is for a very short duration. Stress is difficult for all people, both addicts and non-addicts alike.

There was a woman whose 16-year-old son died in a fire. One year earlier, the same boy was in an almost fatal accident. A van hit him while he rode his bike and left him in a coma. While he awoke from the coma and survived, he suffered permanent brain damage. One year later a fire struck their home. The fire happened because of electrical wiring. The family thought that everyone made it out of the house. They saw their son's dog and thought he was safe as well because he never went anywhere without his dog. The firefighters discovered the boy's badly burned body in his bedroom and informed his parents. His mother seemed to handle the loss well, never losing her composure. Her husband talked of his grief and his anger at

God to anyone who would listen. The mother seemed to handle the loss better than her husband. Within ten years of the anniversary of their son's death, the woman died of cancer and within a year following her death, her husband died. No doubt, the lady who seemed so composed during such unbelievable stressful times and handled it well succumbed to it.

Another example is Patsy Ramsey, the mother of Jon Bonet Ramsey, the six-year-old child pageant star found by her father in their basement murdered. The case made news headlines. The police initially accused the Ramsey's of killing their daughter. Patsy Ramsey experienced unbearable stress from both the grief over the horrible death of her daughter along with the police accusing her of murdering Jon Bonet. They alleged that she wrote the ransom note that the killer left behind. Patsy also public criticism for her placing Jon Bonet in pageants.

About six months before the ten-year anniversary of Jon Bonet's death, Patsy died of ovarian cancer. For individuals who do not turn to substance to deal with life's difficulties, stress affects them through illness and mental disorders, which develop. Substance abusers cannot be lumped into the low tolerance for stress box because stress is hard for everyone. Stress sets off an addict's flight and fright response, and they want to flee from it through their binges. Earlier in the chapter, I stated that an addict does self-medicate their anxiety and will also use their vice as an aid to relieve their tension.

There is the finding that substance abusers are risk takers; again, while they might take chances in some areas, they will not take risks in others. So this is an unfair generalization. Addicts take on danger in pursuit of their escape from their situation. This kicks in the flight and fright response, which causes an addict to take the risks associated with their habit.

Degrees of Addiction

Among addicts, there are varying degrees of addiction. Some start young and others later in life. Career addicts are those who start using at an early age and continue through each decade of their lives until their addiction kills them. Some addicts cannot beat their habit for the life of them. Others find sobriety early in their using career.

Some addicts get clean and sober and others do not. Some of these persons die young from the damage caused by their continuous consumption of substances. This list does not include those who die of overdoses or suicide but whose bodies give way to cirrhosis and other alcohol, and drug induced illnesses. These human garbage cans take all and any substances that come their way. These addicts will take everything and anything that alters their mind.

Every addict has his or her habit or drug of choice. While some will use heroin, others will never touch it. Some will only drink alcohol and will not use drugs. Others prefer cocaine and crack and do not like alcohol, some methamphetamine, others barbiturates. For others, their addiction is food, cigarettes, or sex.

Many addicts suffer from mood swings, depression, and anxiety. These moods lend to the pain an addict feels within himself or herself, which can result from childhood trauma. Some addicts come from loving and supportive families and do not fit the above mold.

Since addicts do not pop out of a box, there is no ready-made formula of personality traits or an exact profile. Addicts come from all lifestyles, from all socio-economic backgrounds; they exist all around the world. What they all have in common is the human condition with all of its faults and frailties. They also have the sin nature and its propensity to give themselves over to the pleasure god.

Dies to Self For The God of Their Vice

An addict who partakes in the use of substance changes dramatically so that their own family members do not know them anymore. Substance abuser's actions grow baser. According to the dictionary, this means that they are "without moral principles; ignoble: "the electorate's baser instincts of greed and selfishness."

According to the Bible, drunkenness is the total opposite of spirituality. It is a sinful state. Addiction brings base actions to the surface. Addicts will steal from their family members, including their own children. Under the influence, they are capable of all kinds of violence including murder. They also commit adulterous or promiscuous acts. Some while intoxicated will even make sexual advances toward their own family members. They are capable of rape and incest.

Addicts pathologically lie, cheat, and steal. While drunk or drugged, they commit acts they never would carry out if they were sober. Such is the case with many criminals who fill prisons.

While sinful behavior is most obvious with substance abuse, each addiction brings out base actions on the part of the addict. Drug abusers will abandon their families, put their children at risk, harm them and commit all kinds of horrible deeds against those they love. Meanwhile, they blame their family members for their addiction and actions. They act as a whirlwind in the lives of their loved ones, causing great emotional harm to their family members. It is as if the substance takes over their entire being. They become irrational, angry, unloving and narcissistic. They, lie, cheat, steal and their lives become all about them.

The Bible talks about the fruits of the spirit as love, joy, peace, patience and admonishes against drunkenness. When an addict is high or drunk, they cares only about themselves. Drunkenness reduces the partaker to all of his or her base and primal emotions. In an attempt to escape, the addict loses him or herself to their addiction.

Dangerous substances deteriorate the user's mind, health, nervous system, and emotions. The substance takes over the addict's life as if it were an invading monster; a body snatcher. What is left is the shell of a person who once existed. An addict becomes selfless throughout their enslavement but not in a good way. They lose the person they once were and become someone whom their family members no longer know.

In the Bible, a Christ following Christian dies to himself and his desires in pursuit of spirituality and a walk with God. An army colonel told me that once he died to himself that he could emerge a warrior and soldier. He considered himself already dead in the face of a horrific battle. He viewed himself as deceased because he felt that there was no way he could survive the gunfire. He believed this thinking helped him survive. The addict dies to his or her spiritual self. What remains is a person who makes their loved ones miserable, who lies, is angry, and commits horrible acts to sustain their addiction.

A substance abuser dies to all three levels of their person: emotionally, spiritually and physically. While physical death does not occur instantly, the self-destructive acts accelerates illnesses that can lead to death. Non-substance addictions also take their toll on a person on all three levels and they too face health risks. Sex addicts are at risk of sexually transmitted diseases. Food addicts risk obesity and other health issues related to their intake of junk foods. Workaholics chance diseases associated with stress. Gamblers also undergo a great deal of stress with the financial ruin they bring on themselves. A woman addicted to running sprinted so much she broke her femur bone. All addicts give their bodies to the god of their vice.

Idolaters

Addicts live for the god of their substance and give this god their time, energy, money and devotion. They discard their lives, their children, and all that is good to pay homage to their idol. An addict is an idolater. God states in the First Commandment of the Ten Commandments, *"you shall have no other god before me."* The substance or vice is the addict's god. Addicts give their heart, soul, children, and money, whatever it takes to have their substance or vice, i.e. their god. Jesus requests that we leave all behind for Him including our families. An addict leaves all behind, including their families, for the god of their substance.

FREE FROM CAPTIVITY

Prisoner

In an attempt to free themselves from their pain addicts become in bondage to their vices. Their obsession controls them, and they become its tireless slave. The god that they give themselves over to rules them like an evil taskmaster. They no longer have control over their lives. The addiction governs them. The addict cannot free him or herself or stop the addiction. What started as pleasure now brings them pain. The vice holds them in their grip and demands all of them. Their lives are not their own, and are lived around their god of substance or of the object of their desire.

Isaiah 61 is the passage that forecasts Jesus' ministry in the realm of having the power to free prisoners. The prisoners he speaks of are addicts. (I elaborate on this passage in some detail in a later chapter.)

Recapping what I discussed so far: an addict has a pleasure button, is a lover of pleasure with intense emotions, and has an inner void and desire to escape. They have obsessive and compulsive thinking, a need to control, have anxiety and or depression, live in denial, blame others and do not take responsibility for their actions and look for any excuse to partake in their vice. Addicts have also died to themselves for the god of their devotion. They are idolaters and slaves or prisoners of their addiction.

Once An Addict Always An Addict

In AA, they say that once an alcoholic always an alcoholic. This also applies to the variety of addictions, substance and non-substance. An alcoholic and a drug addict who get clean and sober will take on new productive vices such as work, exercise, eating right, a relationship, foods, etc. This goes back to the hardwiring of an addict. When things feel good, they feel great and when they feel bad they feel terrible. This is what leads an addict to push their pleasure button and keep their hand on it full throttle.

With every positive, there is a negative. While acting on their compulsion for harmful substances addicts can destroy their lives, this same obsessive behavior can cause them to accomplish some great work that takes lots of focus, dedication and attention. Although there are various vices and different types of addicts, those who get addicted to alcohol and drugs cause the greatest destruction in their lives.

I wrote this book to help addicts understand themselves and provide Biblical secrets to help them break free from their addictions. The first place that an addict must come to is the recognition and admittance that they are an addict. If you have come to admit this, you are ready for the next steps of recovery and deliverance. In the following several chapters, we will look at addictive substances and pastimes, which the alcoholic and drug addict turns to provide them their escape, give them pleasure and help them fill their inner void.

2

ADDICTIVE & MIND-ALTERING DRUGS

The three main drugs of use are cannabis (such as marijuana), opiates (such as heroin), and cocaine. The world of mind altering, psychoactive substances is vast with both legal and illegal substances, well-known to lesser-known drugs. Homemade, pharmaceutical, brewed, concocted, medicines for humans, animals, to dangerous solvents; if it alters one's mind an addict will abuse it regardless of the consequences.

The food that supplies our supermarket shelves does not represent the many varieties of fruits and vegetables available. The groceries that make it to market are the easiest to grow, store, and transport. It is the same in the drug world. Well-known drugs that sell in the streets are the easiest to make, obtain and transfer.

During the past 100 years, advances in chemistry and pharmacology (the science of drugs) have allowed many new drugs. With the advance in medicine comes the progression of the problem of drug dependency because of the plethora of potent and highly addictive drugs. Drug makers processed and refined opium into morphine and heroin. In the mid-1800s coca leaves were processed and refined into cocaine and by the mid-1980s cartel chemists honed it into crack. Drug makers created amphetamines in a laboratory, along with hallucinogenic drugs such as LSD, ecstasy, and MDA. These new pills and refined old drugs are more powerful and addictive than any drugs in the past.

The International Drug Evaluation and Classification Program categorize recreational drugs into seven main categories. The drugs in each category product similar effects in the user, even though they may differ on the way they produce those effects. The major categories include:

The 7 Drug Categories

Drugs from the seven categories affect a person's central nervous system, impair their normal faculties, including the ability to operate a motor vehicle safely.

1. **Central Nervous System (CNS) Depressants** slow down the brain and body and include alcohol, tranquilizers and anti-depressants.
2. **CNS Stimulants** accelerate the heart rate and elevate the blood pressure and "speed-up" or over-stimulate the body. These include Cocaine, "Crack," Amphetamines and Methamphetamine ("Crank").
3. **Hallucinogens** cause the user to perceive things differently than they actually are. Examples include LSD, Peyote, Psilocybin and MDMA (Ecstasy)
4. **Dissociative Anesthetics** inhibit pain by cutting off or dissociating the brain's perception of the pain. PCP is an example of a Dissociative Anesthetics.
5. **Narcotic Analgesics** relieves pain, induces euphoria and creates mood changes in the user. Examples include Opium, Codeine, Heroin, Demerol, Darvon, Morphine, Methadone, Vicodin and OxyContin.
6. **Inhalants** include a wide variety of breathable substances that produce mind-altering results and effects. Examples of inhalants include toluene, plastic cement, paint, gasoline, paint thinners, hair sprays, and various anesthetic gases.

7. **Cannabis** is the scientific name for marijuana. The active ingredient in cannabis is delta-9 tetrahydrocannabinol, or THC. This category includes cannabinoids and synthetics.

The worldwide use of these drugs tops all the other categories of abused drugs combined. For this book, we will further break them down into nine categories and we will discuss each of them including some lesser-known drugs.

This chapter will not provide an exhaustive list of the substances that people abuse but will cover alcohol, mainstream drugs and will mention some lesser-known drugs. We have included nicotine from tobacco, which many who abuse alcohol and drugs also abuse and become addicted to, which classify as drugs.

The Nine Categories

1. Alcohol (ethanol)
2. Nicotine and tobacco
3. Depressants (barbiturates, benzodiazepines)
4. Stimulants (amphetamines, cocaine)
5. Marijuana
6. Opioids (morphine, heroin, methadone)
7. Psychedelics (LSD, mescaline, ecstasy)
8. inhalants (glue, nitrous oxide)
9. Phencyclidine (PCP)

Alcohol: The Universal Substance

According to the World Health Organization's 2004 report on worldwide alcohol use, about 2 billion people drink alcohol with 76.3 million with diagnosable alcohol addiction disorders. From a public health perspective, alcohol consumption's health and social consequences create a global burden and is considerable in most parts of the world. In addition to causing diseases in heavy users, alcohol contributes to the cause of death and disability for the world's youth. Alcohol use plays a role in more than 60 types of disease and injury. Alcohol contributes to an increase in alcohol-related disease, accidental deaths, domestic violence, rape, murder, manslaughter, and other crimes. In the United States, excessive alcohol use is the third leading lifestyle-related cause of death for people in the United States each year.

Alcohol is the universal intoxicant. Brewers make it from everything and anything. Some desperate alcoholics will drink mouthwash and poisonous cosmetic products because alcohol is an ingredient.

In Kenya in November of 2000, 140 people died and many went blind while hundreds were hospitalized after consuming poisonous, and illegal liquor called *kumi kumi*. Made from sorghum, maize or millet, the alcoholic drink is common among Kenyans living in the country's poor and rural areas. *Kumi kumi* contains methanol and other dangerous additives such as car battery acid and formalin.

In Zimbabwe, kachasu, a home-distilled brew, is a major problem in the country and causes poisonings due to the use of lethal additives to increase its effects.

Country liquor is a distilled alcoholic beverage made from locally available sugarcane, rice, palm, coconut and cheap grains. Adulteration is common; industrial methylated spirit, an adulterant, occasionally causes mass poisonings with drinkers losing their lives or suffering permanent eye damage. Illicit liquor's cheap price is popular among the poor.

In India, homemade liquor production and its marketing is mainstream. Alcoholic beverages are made from a variety of fruits, and grains. Indigenous Venezuela tribes make corn liquor. They hollow out the trunk of a tree and fill it with corn mash. Once it ferments, it produces an alcoholic cocktail with a very high alcohol content.

In the East Malaysian states of Sabah and Sarawak on the island of Borneo, the natives drink a potent homemade rice wine called *tuak* or *tapai*. In Uganda, *Tonto* is the traditional brew, and it is made from special varieties of bananas. In central Uganda it is called *mwenge bigere*. In Uganda, banana growing is a major agricultural activity and banana booze is plentiful.

Recipe for Tonto

Ingredients
Green banana's that have ripened for three to five days.
Grass
Roasted and Ground Sorghum
Water

Directions
Place bananas in a warmed pit lined with banana leaves. Squeeze Juice (a group of men using their feet with spear grass accomplishes the task).
Filter juice through grass held in calabash funnel diluted with water. Add roasted and ground sorghum to the diluted banana juice using a canoe-shaped wood container. Cover the fermented broth with banana leaves, split banana stems in a warmed pit, and incubate for 2-4 days. The alcohol content in *tonto* ranges between 6 and 11% and is consumed from small gourds using straws.

In Botswana, *Bojalwa* (sorghum beer) and *khadi* are both home-brewed beer-like drinks that vary greatly in terms of taste, consistency and alcohol content. Brewers make a base or 'mash' consisting of a combination of any of the following ingredients: wild berries, pumpkins, roots, oranges, sorghum and maize. Sometimes they mix yeast, black tobacco or other unspecified substances to give it 'strength', and there have been rumors of car battery acid also being added.

In Ethiopia, they drink *Talla,* an Ethiopian home-brewed beer made with barley or wheat, hops, or spices. It has a smoky flavor due to the addition of bread darkened by baking and use of a fermentation vessel, smoked by inversion over smoldering wood.

In Egypt, *Bouza* (traditional beer) is a fermented alcoholic beverage produced from wheat in Egypt, and the Egyptians have brewed *Bouza* since the days of the Pharaohs. It is a thick, pasty yellow beverage and produces a sensation of heat when consumed. *Bouza* has a very short shelf life of about a day.

In Ghana, *Pito* (local brew made from millet) is widely consumed in Ghana. Its taste varies from slightly sweet to very sour. There are four types of *Pito* in Ghana –*nandom*, *kokmba*, *togo* and *dagarti*. The differences lie in their extraction and fermentation methods.

In Kenya, *Muratina* is an alcoholic drink made from sugar cane and muratina fruit in Kenya. The fruit is cut in half, sun dried and boiled in water. The water is removed and the fruit sun-dried again. They mix fruit with a small amount of sugar-cane juice and incubated in a warm place. The fruit is removed from the juice after 24 hours and sun-dried. They add fruit to a barrel of sugar-cane juice and ferment for between one and four days. The drink has a sour alcoholic taste.

Prisoners make alcohol in prisons. One prison recipe called *Pruno* uses oranges, fruit cocktail, sugar cubes, ketchup, and hot water. Its flavor tastes like a "vomit wine cooler."

Where there is grain, fruit, sugar or fruit sugar, there is alcohol. While some of these drinks do not sound palatable, alcoholics do not drink for taste, they drink to get drunk.

Dangerous Ingredients of Home Brews

The home brews of some of these countries use dangerous ingredients. According to the World Health Organization, a study that collected and analyzed 15 homemade and commercially available alcoholic beverages in Tanzania found that alcohol concentrations of two distilled samples contained three to ten times the amount of ethanol. Chemists found aflatoxin thiamine, a mycotoxin due to the use of contaminated grains or fruit for their production. The amount of zinc in four samples was double the World Health Organization recommended maximum for drinking water. One brewed beverage contained toxic amounts of manganese. Both distilled spirits were rich in fusel alcohols and one contained caffeine. Traditional alcoholic brews contain impurities and contaminants, which pose severe health risks, including carcinogens.

Physical Dependence

Alcohol is a sedative-hypnotic drug that acts in the brain like other drugs of its class such as barbiturates and benzodiazepine tranquilizers. Alcohol, like barbs and benzos can cause physical dependence in anyone who drinks enough for any length of time.

The withdrawal symptoms of alcohol are identical to drugs in the same class such as Valium and Xanax. Withdrawal symptoms include:

Anxiety, restlessness, irritability, and insomnia
Elevated blood pressure, temperature, pulse, and respiration
Confusion and disorientation
Visual and auditory hallucinations, acute psychotic behavior
Grand mal seizures
Infrequently sudden death

Alcoholics cannot use their willpower to stop drinking. Their craving for alcohol is so great that it hinders their ability to discontinue drinking.

Nicotine Tobacco

Nicotine is the second class of most abused substances and many people do not consider nicotine a drug, but a habit. Nicotine is a drug and while its mind-altering effects seem subtle, it is a drug nonetheless. Most addicts use it along with other substances as if it is a link in the chain of addictive drugs. A study found that nicotine exposure in adolescent mice retards the growth of the dopamine system, thus increasing the risk of substance abuse. Scientists think this might explain why addicts smoke along with consuming other addictive substances such as caffeine, alcohol and other drugs and why it is a link in the substance abuse chain.

The World Health Organization estimates that at least one-third of the global adult population, or 1.1 billion people aged 15 years and older, smoked cigarettes in the early 1990s. There are more smokers in developing poorer third-world nations. In wealthier industrialized countries, more women smoke than women in banana republics. In all categories, more men smoke than women. Tobacco use has increased in these emerging markets and is epidemic among children and pre-teens. Most tobacco use starts during childhood and adolescence with the numbers of its use among children worldwide increasing.

According to the WHO, "A long-term tobacco user has a 50% chance of dying prematurely from tobacco-caused disease. In 1990, tobacco accounted for nearly a quarter of all male deaths and 7% of all female deaths worldwide, including more than 40% of fatalities among men in formerly socialist areas. Tobacco-related diseases shortened the lives of affected smokers by an average of 16 years."

Tobacco Products Are Highly Addictive

Cigarette companies formulate cigarettes to undermine efforts to stop using them and to hook the user into addiction. Chemists working for tobacco companies treat the tobacco with addictive substances such as white sugar and chocolate liquor. Quitting smoking seems impossible for the majority of cigarette smokers. They become a struggle to overcome. Most smokers will tell you that they love to smoke and do not want to quit smoking despite knowing all the health risks.

Nicotine inhaled through smoking passes quickly through the arterial blood stream and into the brain, resulting in intense effects in the central nervous system. Nicotine levels drop between cigarettes.

Many who smoke do not consider nicotine a drug because it does not have any effects of inebriation and intoxication of other drugs. Although subtle, nicotine is mood altering and is both a stimulant and a relaxant. Nicotine's addictive effects are similar to amphetamines. Nicotine activates reward pathways—the circuitry within the brain that regulates feelings of pleasure and euphoria.

Dopamine is one of the brain's key neurotransmitters. Nicotine increases the levels of dopamine within the brain's reward circuits, making it highly addictive. Nicotine is more habit forming than cocaine and heroin. Like other physically dependent drugs, nicotine withdrawal causes down-regulation of the production of dopamine and other stimulatory neurotransmitters as the brain attempts to compensate for artificial stimulation. Nicotine increases reward pathway sensitivity, which means that you will look for something to replace it such as eating comfort foods upon quitting. Cocaine and heroin are the opposite and reduce reward pathway sensitivity, which means that nothing that replaces the reward feels the same as the drug. This neuronal brain alteration persists for months after quitting. Nicotine also can cause addiction in animals.

The effects of smoking withdrawal last for a month, which makes quitting very difficult. Withdrawal symptoms following during the early days and weeks of stopping include cravings and urges to smoke, difficulty concentrating, nervousness, restlessness, irritability, anxiety, cognitive impairment, increased appetite and (eventually) weight gain.

Depressants (Barbiturates, Benzodiazepines)

Barbiturates rank among the most widely prescribed, used and abused drugs throughout the world. Fifteen members within this group sell in the United States, and about 20 additional benzodiazepines retail in other countries. Pharmacies filled an estimated 600 million prescriptions for minor tranquilizers in U.S. pharmacies alone. Barbiturates depress the central nervous system delivering a sedative effect. They produce mild sedation or coma depending upon the dosage. Benzodiazepines are used therapeutically to sedate, induce sleep, relieve anxiety and muscle spasms, and to prevent seizures.

Patients who have difficulty falling asleep and do not have anxiety use short-acting benzodiazepines. The shorter-acting benzodiazepines used to manage insomnia include estazolam (ProSom®), flurazepam (Dalmane®), temazepam (Restoril®), and triazolam (Halcion®). Midazolam (Versed®), is used for sedation, anxiety, and amnesia in critical care settings and prior to anesthesia and is injected.

Benzodiazepines with a longer duration of action treat insomnia in patients with anxiety. These benzodiazepines include alprazolam (Xanax®), chlordiazepoxide (librium®), clorazepate (Tranxene®), diazepam (Valium®), halazepam (Paxipam®), lorazepam (Ativan®), oxazepam (Serax®), prazepam (Centrax®), and quazepam (Doral®). Clonazepam (Klonopin®), diazepam, and clorazepate are also used as anticonvulsants.

Repeated use of large doses along with daily use of therapeutic doses is associated with amnesia, hostility, irritability, and vivid or disturbing dreams. The body needs a higher dose to get the same effect. Benzodiazepines are also highly addictive. The withdrawal from benzos is similar to that of alcohol and may require hospitalization. Tapering down the dose eliminates many of the withdrawal symptoms.

Stimulants (Amphetamines, Cocaine)

Amphetamines are stimulant drugs, which produce increased wakefulness and focus along with decreased fatigue and appetite. Brand names amphetamines include Adderall, Dexedrine, Dextrostat, Desoxyn, ProCentra, and Vyvanse, as well as Benzedrine in the past. Recreational users of amphetamines most commonly refer to the drug as "speed."

Throughout the 1990s, the use of amphetamines increased dramatically worldwide. The main regions manufacturing and using them are in North America, Western Europe, and Asia. By the end of the 1990s, stimulant use increased in Asia and stabilized or declined in North America and Western Europe. Asia is the leading region for use and manufacture of stimulants.

The production of amphetamines is a worldwide problem. They can are often manufactured wherever the chemicals to make them are available in illegal laboratories. The pharmaceutical companies in a few countries in South America and Africa produce amphetamines for medicinal use. Amphetamine-type stimulant production is difficult to control because of the wide range of "upper" drugs available. In some countries, a chemical variation of a particular amphetamine-type stimulant compound can create a new pill that is legal.

Tolerance develops rapidly with amphetamine abuse, and the user needs increasing amounts of the drug in order to achieve the same effect.

Methamphetamine

The monster of all drugs falls into this category and it is the one that causes the greatest damage in the body. It literally destroys the insides of the user. It is also the most addictive: methamphetamine.

Methamphetamine is a central nervous system stimulant and is a Schedule II drug meaning it is available only through a prescription with no refills. Although doctors prescribe methamphetamine, it has limited medical uses, and doctors recommend it only in small doses.

Drug makers manufacture methamphetamine in foreign or domestic super labs, and in small, illegal laboratories. Its production endangers the people in the labs, neighbors, and the environment. Making illegal meth can cause explosions that resemble bomb blasts.

Methamphetamine is a white, odorless, bitter-tasting crystalline powder that easily dissolves in water or alcohol. The user takes it orally, by snorting, needle injection, or by smoking. The effects of methamphetamine are far more intense than cocaine or crack because the effects last longer and it causes the brain to release massive amounts of dopamine.

Cocaine

Cocaine comes from the leaves of the coca plant. The name comes from "coca" in addition to the alkaloid suffix -ine, forming cocaine. It is a central nervous system stimulant, an appetite suppressant, and a topical anesthetic.

Worldwide, two-thirds of all countries report cocaine use. North America, with declining rates, still leads the world. In Western Europe, cocaine use has steadily risen since the early 1980s. Cocaine intake is lowest in Asia. Cocaine consumption is higher in affluent countries. According to an article in Spiegel Online International by Markus Becker, New York is the cocaine capital of the world with Europe catching up. Spain is in the lead and the British and Italians not far behind. African rates of cocaine use are low as they generally show more amphetamine-type stimulant use than use of opium and cocaine.

The leading countries that grow coca and produce cocaine are Bolivia, Peru, and Colombia. North American countries are the main market for cocaine because of easy access to South America. These countries yield metric tons of coca worth an estimated $134 million. Bolivia produced 70 tons of coca valued at $63 million. For poor countries, these dollar amounts are worth the risks and even government officials take part in the trade.

Cocaine is a serotonin–norepinephrine–dopamine reuptake inhibitor, which affects the function of these neurotransmitters as an outside or added transporter molecule. Because of the way it affects the dopamine reward pathway, cocaine is addictive. Cocaine, both in powder form and as crack, is an extremely habit forming stimulant. An addict usually loses interest in many areas of life, including school, sports, family, and friends.

Chronic cocaine-use causes a decrease in the production of enkephalin, one of the brain's natural opioids. This in turn causes a compensatory increase in the number of mu-receptors. The number of unoccupied mu-receptors may be associated with the craving and abstinence syndrome. After chronic exposure to cocaine, the central nervous system reduces the number of dopamine receptors. The amount of dopamine transporter protein increases.

What this means is that the normal things in life that make one feel pleasure no longer help the addict to feel good. Their brain now requires the drug to feel enjoyment. This change in brain chemistry happens with most drugs. A study came out that showed that even internet addiction alters brain chemistry. This report took brain changes out of the realm of substance abuse and into the arena of addictions in general.

Tolerance develops relatively modestly. While the cocaine-user still gets high; in the absence of cocaine, his pre-synaptic neurons seize dopamine in the synaptic cleft with greater efficiency. This induces depression, and profound despair. No cocaine user ever feels content after taking cocaine. They just want more.

Marijuana

Cannabis, also known as marijuana, is a psychoactive drug and a medicine. Cannabis, one of the most widely used drugs in the world, produces effects similar to low doses of classic psychedelics. In high doses it can be quite psychedelic, depending on the strain. The major compound in cannabis is THC, which is one of 400 compounds in the plant including other cannabinoids, which can produce sensory effects unlike the psychoactive effects of THC.

THC is a mind-altering drug, which affects people's mood and feelings. THC is also a depressant, meaning that it slows the brain down. It can make someone feel sedated and sleepy and is considered a mild hallucinogenic, distorting their perception, senses and reality. Colors can seem brighter or darker, and a new meaning and details into things emerge. Those who use it refer to the feelings it causes as being stoned.

Cannabis remains the most widely used drug worldwide. Marijuana use is increasing, but in some parts of the globe, notably North America, Russia, China, and parts of Asia, use has stabilized or decreased in recent years. The United Nations' World Drug Report estimates that cannabis is the most widely abused substance in all parts of the world, with around 141 million people using it.

According to the National Survey on Drug Use and Health, in 2009, 16.7 million Americans aged 12 or older used marijuana at least once in the month prior to being surveyed, an increase over the rates reported in all years that decade. There was also a significant increase among youth and young adults aged 12-25.

For the addict, they feel that they are not alone because everyone is doing it, at least everyone in their circles because like finds like. Sadly, even born-again Christian groups have come out saying that there is nothing wrong with marijuana use.

Cannabis is the most widely used drug because the crop grows in many different climates and requires no processing for use, which is why it is nicknamed weed. Of the 196 countries that are on the earth, more than 120 nations reported cannabis growing. The major growers and suppliers of cannabis for the world market are Morocco, South Africa, Nigeria, Afghanistan, Pakistan, Mexico, Colombia, and Jamaica.

A trend in cannabis cultivation is hydroponics and other indoor growing techniques. The improved methods yield a plant with a much higher concentration of THC, its active ingredient. The marijuana from these crops is far more powerful than the cannabis smoked in the 1960s and 1970s. For poor countries, the economic value of cannabis is significant. Some experts consider marijuana a gateway drug, which means it is a door to addictive substances. Marijuana is not physically habit-forming.

Opioids (Morphine, Heroin, Methadone)

Opiates are nature's painkillers. The Bible states that the plants will be for medicine and there is no greater painkiller on earth than opiates. Those who have suffered injuries in accidents, undergone surgery, or suffered from cancer benefit from the pain-relieving abilities of opiates. They work effectively on reducing excruciating physical pain.

Opiates work by targeting the opiate receptors in the brain, to which they attach themselves. These receptors are responsible for pain. The human body uses these receptor sites to bind with endorphins, which are the body's natural pain-relieving chemicals. Endorphins are our body's feel-good chemicals, which help the body dull feelings of pain. They also make us feel good. Endorphins aid in normal body functions, including hormone regulation and respiration.

The brain receptors trigger systems within the body to modify operation. This includes the respiratory centers, which react by reducing the breathing rate. Opiates also work in the spinal cord by blocking the transmission of pain messages between the neurons and brain. Medicine refers to this process as "analgesia." Opiates quickly activate the brain's reward system and increase the production of dopamine and create a "rush" feeling.

Opiates are highly addictive. The National Institute of Health states, "When opiates are prescribed by a physician for the treatment of pain and are taken in the prescribed dosage, they are safe, and there is little chance of addition." When an opiate is used "improperly," however, it can "quickly trigger addition."

Withdrawal symptoms includes muscle aches, insomnia, sweating, anxiety and intensity of any physical pain. Late withdrawal symptoms progress to diarrhea, cramping and vomiting.

The opium poppy plant produces opiates. The plant grows in many countries around the world. The principal growing areas for opium poppies are in Southwest Asia (Afghanistan and Pakistan), Southeast Asia (Laos or Lao People's Democratic Republic, Myanmar, Thailand, and Vietnam), and Latin America (Colombia and Mexico). According to the WHO in 1999, Afghanistan accounted for 79 percent of world opium production, Myanmar produced 15 percent of the world opium, and other nations produced the remaining 6 percent. The highest level of abuse is in Southwest and Southwest Asia where opium grows.

The use of opiates has been rising worldwide at an alarming rate, with more than two-thirds of the countries in the world reporting increases. Opiate use is highest in developing nations, while use in wealthy nations is stable or declining. Opium production has increased dramatically and has shifted from Southeast Asia to Southwest Asia with Afghanistan leading the world in the opium trade. The country makes 79 percent of the world's opium. Opiate drugs are most widely used in Asia. Opiate use is much lower in North America, Central America, South America, and Europe than it is in Asia.

Purdue Pharma introduced Oxicontin in 1995. It became a pill substitute for heroin among drug users and started the prescription painkiller epidemic. Prescription painkiller use is on the rise. According to Reuters, "Prescription drug abuse is the new scourge of rural America. It now leads to more deaths in the United States than heroin and cocaine combined."

Psychedelics (LSD, mescaline, ecstasy)

A psychedelic substance is a psychoactive drug whose primary action is to alter cognition and perception. Psychedelics are part of a wider class of drugs known as hallucinogens, a category that also includes related substances such as dissociatives and deliriants. Psychedelics cause the user to hallucinate and distort sights and sounds. Medicine uses psychedelics to promote physical and mental healing. Tribal communities use them in pagan religious festivals and ceremonies. Known as entheogens, Native American practitioners using mescaline-containing cacti such as Peyote have reported success against alcoholism. Mazatec practitioners routinely use psilocybin mushrooms for divination and healing. Ayahuasca, a psychotropic drug, is still used in Peru for religious festivals.

Mescaline is one of the oldest psychedelics known to man. It is the major active component of the small dumpling cactus known as Peyote. It grows wild in the Southwestern United

FREE FROM CAPTIVITY

States and in Northern Mexico. It is used in a number of religious traditions among the native Indians of these areas. The cactus has the botanical name of Lophophora williamsii or Anhalonium lewinii and is immediately recognizable by its small round shape and the appearance of tufts of soft fuzz in place of the more conventional spines. The dried plant material has been classically used with anywhere from a few to a couple of dozen of the hard tops, called buttons, being consumed during their ceremonies.

Classic psychedelics include LSD also called acid, a semi-synthetic psychedelic derived from ergot and discovered by the late Albert Hoffman in 1938 and noted for its psychoactive properties later in 1943. There are various classes of psychedelics, and among them are DMT, and mescaline.

Most users report that the two families have different qualities in the "feel" of the experience, which are hard to describe. At lower doses, these include sensory alterations, such as the warping of surfaces, shape suggestibility, and color variations. Users report vivid colors that they have not previously seen, and repetitive geometric shapes are common. Higher doses often cause intense and alterations of sensory perception, such as the visions of additional spatial or temporal dimensions. The drugs vary considerably. For instance, 5-MeO-DMT rarely produces the visual effects typical of other psychedelics. Some drugs, such as the β-carbolines, cause differing effects from the more standard types of psychedelics.

The drug ecstasy falls under the class of psychedelics. Their effects are characterized by feelings of openness, euphoria, empathy, love, heightened self-awareness, and by mild visual distortions. MDA is atypical to this experience, often causing hallucinations and psychedelic effects, but with substantially less mental involvement, and is possibly both a serotonin releaser and 5-HT$_{2A}$ receptor agonist. This gives the user, subjectively, the best from both worlds.

There are the dissociative psychedelics such as ketamine, which produces sensations of their spirit disconnecting from their body. Their surrounding environment is unreal. Ketamine is an anesthetic in veterinary and pediatric medicine. Along with being a powerful, hallucinogenic it relieves pain.

As an anesthetic, the liquid it is injected. Some users inject it and some allow the liquid to evaporate, and snort the white substance. Injection allows the user to feel its effects immediately, while snorting takes the user 5-15 minutes to feel its effects.

Many regular drug users consider ketamine the "first addictive psychedelic they have ever encountered." Psychedelic drug use tends to magnify and increase the emotional state of the user. Users of ketamine develop a tolerance to it. Bodily, tolerance rises quickly with regular use and lasts for about three days. Taking the same dose of Special K during this period means you will not get the effect you are looking for. Frequent users require increasing doses and many report a diminishing of the ketamine high over time, so that the effect becomes more like a combination of cocaine and cannabis.

Chronic users - mainly those who inject - develop something close to permanent tolerance so, after months of use, are unable to experience the psychedelic effects ever again.

Kit Kat is a drug that creates a psychological dependence. After taking ketamine for a while, you will associate the drug with pleasurable experiences. Abstinence produces emotional withdrawal symptoms, such as depression, irritability, and insomnia.

Ketamine does not appear to produce physical withdrawal symptoms in chronic users. There are anecdotal reports of tension, twitchiness, poor attention span, and restlessness in abstinent long-term users, but this may be due more to the sedative norketamine (a breakdown product of ketamine) lingering in the blood stream.

There is also salvia divinorum, which has extremely disorienting effects, complete loss of reality-perception and users seeing their consciousness as being housed in different objects, i.e. a pane of glass or a pencil.

FREE FROM CAPTIVITY

Marijuana is the most widely used psychedelic. Other psychedelics like Ketamine and Ecstasy are fad drugs that become popular with adolescents or make it into the club scene.

Inhalants (Glue, Nitrous Oxide)

Inhalants are among items that we have within our households. They are substances that are inhaled to give the user an immediate head rush or high. Items such as glue, deodorant, paint thinners alter a person's mind, and these substances are so dangerous they can result in death.

Nitrous oxide, commonly known as laughing gas, which dentists use for its anesthetic and analgesic effects, is also an inhalant that drug users abuse for its euphoric effects.

According to Maxim W. Furek, MA, CAC who wrote the article, "The Silent Killer: Inhalant Abuse:"

"... huffing, the practice of inhaling chemical fumes into the lungs... is widespread with adolescent's ages 12 to 17 and, according to the Partnership for a Drug-Free America, one child in five, in grades 7 through 12, has tried sniffing fumes of legal household goods (National Inhalant Prevention Coalition (NIPC), 2001). Most of the abusers are in the 12-14 age group (Cersonsky, 2000). Since 1975, Monitoring the Future has documented a lifetime incidence of inhalant abuse with high school seniors as high as 15 to 20 percent (NIDA, 1994)."

Inhalant use plagues predominantly white children, followed by Hispanic, and comparatively few African-American children. Cindi Bookout, executive director for the Alliance for Consumer Education, states, "One of the greatest concerns voiced by parents, teachers, and community leaders is that of inhalant abuse. ... In the past decade, it has nearly doubled. According to the American Association of Pediatrics, almost 21 percent of all eighth graders have tried some form of inhalants. Among 12 year olds, inhalants are the most frequently used illicit substance."

Phencyclidine (PCP)

PCP, or phencyclidine, is a "dissociative" anesthetic that scientists developed in the 1950s for surgery. Its sedative and anesthetic effects are trance-like, and patients experience a feeling of being "out of body" and detached from their environment. Doctors discontinued using PCP for surgeries in 1965, because patients became agitated, delusional, and irrational while recovering from its anesthetic effects.

PCP on the street sells in tablets, capsules, and colored powders or liquid. Drug maker's ad it to a leafy material such as mint, parsley, oregano, tobacco, or marijuana. PCP can be snorted, smoked, injected, or swallowed. Unbeknownst to drug users, drug dealers add PCP to marijuana, LSD, or methamphetamine. PCP is addicting. According to the National Drug Intelligence Center, "Individuals of all ages use PCP. Data reported in the National Household Survey on Drug Abuse indicate that an estimated 6 million U.S. residents aged 12 and older used PCP at least once in their lifetime. Individuals of all ages use PCP." The survey also revealed that many teenagers and young adults use PCP. Its use among high-school students is a particular concern. More than 3 percent of high school seniors in the United States sampled the drug at least one time, and more than 1 percent used PCP in the past year, according to the University of Michigan's Monitoring the Future Survey.

This concludes the list of dangerous substances, their addiction potential and their widespread use. In the next chapter, "The Getting High Illusion," we will look at these substances in more detail and from an eye-opening perspective.

3

THE GETTING HIGH ILLUSION

Addicts are under the illusion that when they take a drink or a drug, the substance gives them a high, as if it contains magical chemicals that cause you to feel better or happy. They think the drug works by its addition into the body and not by altering the brain's chemistry. Most substances, especially the dangerous, addictive substances, work by short circuiting your own bodies' chemistry. The "high" isn't chemical induced elation, but a change in your brain and body make-up.

"Getting wasted" is really about using a drug that alters your brain chemistry by releasing its feel-good chemicals so that you no longer feel, or you hallucinate. The drug does not allow you to see things; rather your brain chemistry is altered and reshuffled so that your perception of time and space malfunctions. The substance rearranges your brain molecules. So what you sniff, smoke, snort, swallow or shoot does not give an experience to you or add to your body, but rather it reorganizes your bodies feel good compounds and in so doing, damages you in the process.

Drugs medically work to treat pain or emotional pain by attempting to correct brain chemistry. If you are a person who is looking for a thrill or an experience by doing drugs, you will not experience a high but rather the reshuffling the above paragraphs describe. Thus, getting high is an allusion to the addict. While this illusion is obvious in the substance category, it also exists for all other vices as well. Many substances also cause negative effects to the body's organs and systems.

We will look at the seven categories from the previous chapter and focus specifically on their effects on the body and what actually happens when you ingest them.

1. Alcohol (ethanol)
2. Nicotine and tobacco
3. Depressants (barbiturates, benzodiazepines)
4. Stimulants (amphetamines, cocaine)
5. Marijuana
6. Opioids (morphine, heroin, methadone)
7. Psychedelics (LSD, mescaline, ecstasy)
8. Inhalants (glue, nitrous oxide)
9. Phencyclidine (PCP)

Alcohol

People drink to relax or to unwind, to have fun, to calm themselves down, to forget their miseries, to help them become more social. For an alcoholic or an addict, every reason is a reason to indulge.

Most feel that when they take a drink, they will feel better and forget their pain. You start to feel good, and you want more. When you are at the point that you should stop, you have lost all ability to think clearly and logically, and you drink yourself into feeling sick or into a blackout. Addicts think of being drunk in a good sense because for them it means that they can escape themselves and their pain.

Alcohol affects the central nervous system, which controls a range of vital body functions, including speech, muscles, sense, organs and sweat glands. Alcohol impairs central nervous system functioning. This impairment is what one refers to as being "drunk." Alcohol inebriation causes unsteady balance, slurred speech, blurred vision, excess sweating and the dulling of the sensation of pain.

FREE FROM CAPTIVITY

Drunkenness closely resembles a stroke. According to the Rush University Medical Center, the symptoms of a stroke are as follows:

- Change in alertness (including sleepiness, unconsciousness, and coma)
- Changes in hearing
- Changes in taste
- Changes that effect touch and the ability to feel pain, pressure, or different temperatures
- Clumsiness
- Confusion or loss of memory
- Difficulty swallowing
- Difficulty writing or reading
- Dizziness or abnormal feeling of movement (vertigo)
- Lack of control over the bladder or bowels
- Loss of balance
- Loss of coordination
- Muscle weakness in the face, arm, or leg (usually just one one side)
- Numbness or tingling on one side of the body
- Personality, mood, or emotional changes
- Problems with eyesight, including decreased vision, double vision, or total loss of vision
- Trouble speaking or understanding others who are speaking
- Trouble walking

One would think that they were reading the signs of drunkenness other than the muscle weakness usually being on one side. When someone drinks, alcohol brings on symptoms similar to a stroke.

In addition to drunkenness producing a self-induced stroke, alcohol also affects the outer layer of the brain (the frontal cortex) that is concerned with conscious thought. This is why people under the influence of alcohol lose their inhibitions. They say and do things they would not do or say while sober.

Alcohol is a diuretic, encouraging the body to lose more water than it takes on by halting the production of the body's anti-diuretic hormone. You feel the need to pee excessively, thus speeding up the loss of fluid from the body that leads to dehydration. Alcohol also attacks our stores of vitamins and minerals, which need to be in the correct balance for the body to function normally. Dehydration caused by drinking can affect the balance by draining potassium from the body, resulting in thirst, muscle cramps, dizziness, and faintness.

When a person drinks, they take in large quantities of increased glucose. Their body responds to this by producing more insulin, which removes the glucose. Once the process has started, the insulin continues removing glucose from the blood. Low blood sugar is responsible for the shakes, excess sweating, dizziness, blurred vision, and tiredness. Drinking lowers blood sugar and brings on a hypoglycemic attack.

The liver is the main organ that gets rid of alcohol by breaking it down. It metabolizes about 90% of the alcohol in our body while only about 10% excretes through either our urine or breath. The liver metabolizes alcohol at the rate of one to two units per hour, sometimes less than that in women. As the body breaks down alcohol, the liver produces more toxins. The liver needs water to rid poisons from the body. Alcohol is a diuretic, and it depletes the body of the water the liver needs to eliminate toxins. To compensate the liver takes water from other organs including the brain, this causes the throbbing headaches.

When the liver is metabolizing alcohol, it produces acetaldehyde, a substance which has toxic effects on our liver, brain and stomach lining, resulting in severe headache, nausea, vomiting and heartburn.

Alcohol upsets sleeping patterns. The dehydration from drinking contributes to insomnia. Alcohol also relaxes the muscles at the back of your mouth, causing snoring. It irritates the stomach triggering gastritis, and vomiting. It produces inflammation in the esophagus, which leads to throat cancers and esophageal hemorrhage. Alcohol also brings on diarrhea because alcohol interferes with the intestine's reabsorption of salt and water.

According to the World Health Organization's Global Status Report on Alcohol published in 2004:

> Alcohol use causes a wide range of physical, mental and social harms. Most health professionals agree that alcohol affects practically every organ in the human body. Alcohol consumption links to more than 60 diseases. These include cancer, *esophageal and liver cancers*: Alcohol use increases the risk of cancer of the mouth (lip, tongue), larynx, salivary glands, esophagus and liver and even stomach, colon, and other cancers. In addition, it causes high blood pressure, stroke, diabetes, coronary heart disease and cirrhosis of the liver. Not to mention alcoholism causes depression and exacerbates personality disorders and mental conditions. Alcohol also causes insomnia.

WHO also found that "higher volume of consumption is associated with more symptoms of depression, in other words, the more you drink as an alcoholic, the more depressed you will become. They found that active alcoholics are more despondent than the rest of the population. For the alcoholic who begins to drink regularly because his or her life is difficult and depressing, they are about to make their lives worse by drinking. Ironically, most alcoholics will call drinking partying and having a good time.

These findings can indicate that alcoholics are depressed to begin with, which is also a factor because of an alcoholic's sensitivity or past trauma. However, alcohol will always make any depression or situation more difficult. This was also found by WHO's researchers and their report stated, "There is sufficient evidence that abstinence substantially removes depressive symptoms in alcohol-dependent persons within a short time frame."

Jeff Herten MD, a former high functioning alcoholic who wrote the book "The Sobering Truth," superbly explains the horrific effects of alcohol in the body. In his book, he states:

> "Alcohol is unusual in that it is absorbed right through the mucosae, the lining of your mouth, esophagus and stomach. It is such a small molecule that it doesn't have to be broken down by any digestive enzymes and thus passes directly through the wall of any portion of the gut. Most foods are large, complex molecules that must be broken down into smaller molecular fragments by stomach acid or by digestive enzymes in the mouth or small intestine to be absorbed. Absorption of alcohol begins immediately after that first swallow and unlike many foods and most medications, alcohol is 100% absorbed into the blood stream, quickly and evenly distributed to all organs of the body, muscles, fat, and, of course, the brain.
>
> Since alcohol is so simple chemically, the body assimilates it very quickly. Its small size and simple structure allows it to pass readily through the membrane of every cell in the body. Alcohol functions as a two-carbon sugar, so it is considered to be in the carbohydrate family. It is metabolized preferentially over glucose in the liver, converted to a chemical called acetaldehyde at a fixed rate of one ounce per hour. Acetaldehyde is a toxic, cancer-causing chemical, and it is the toxicity that is responsible for a large portion of the damage alcohol does to the body. The higher the blood alcohol, the higher the acetaldehyde concentration.
>
> Alcohol is a cell poison. At high concentrations it interferes with normal cell metabolism and is toxic to many cells in the body, including the liver, heart, and nervous system. Alcohol is a toxin, even worse it as a neurotoxin because it can poison the brain."

When one ingests alcohol, they are actually taking in a neurotoxin. Think of all the deadly nerve gases that cause all kinds of horrors to the nervous system, and you have got alcohol a substance, which many people willingly ingest, for the getting drunk or high illusion. When you drink alcohol, you are poisoning yourself, ingesting a neurotoxin all for the sake of a relaxation or escape that ends up biting you in the end like a snake.

Nicotine

When one smokes a cigarette, they enjoy the smoke as they inhale it and exhale. To the smoker, the cigarette relaxes them and is a habit they relish. All smokers are under the illusion that they have developed a habit and are not under the influence of a drug. Nicotine is not a habit; it is a drug. Nicotine stimulates the release of many chemical messengers including acetylcholine, norepinephrine, epinephrine, vasopressin, arginine, dopamine, autocine agents and beta-endorphin.

Nicotine makes the user feel sharp, calm and alert because it enhances alertness, concentration and memory and reduces pain and anxiety. Nicotine also extends the duration and positive effects of dopamine and increases sensitivity of brain reward systems. Like other stimulants, it reduces the appetite and raises metabolism. Within seven seconds of taking a drag of a cigarette, the release of neurotransmitters and hormones produce nicotine's effects.

The rapid delivery of nicotine in the brain allows the smoker to regulate the dose of nicotine from a cigarette to achieve specific psychoactive effects. Smokers use the nicotine from smoked tobacco as a form of affect modulation or regulation. During times of abstinence, a smoker will experience depression.

For a stimulating effect, smokers take short quick puffs, which produce a low level of blood nicotine and stimulate nerve transmission. During relaxation, deep puffs produce a high level of blood nicotine, which depresses the passage of nerve impulses producing a mild sedative effect. At low doses, nicotine potently enhances the actions of norepinephrine and dopamine within the brain, causing a drug effect typical of stimulants. At higher doses, nicotine enhances the effect of serotonin and opiate activity, producing a calming, pain-killing effect. Nicotine is unique compared to most drugs because it changes from stimulant to sedative-painkiller in increasing dosages and use.

Nicotine affects so many neurotransmitters that they become near impossible to quit. A smoker's enjoyment of their habit is really an addiction to the chemicals released into the brain from smoking.

Cigarette smoking causes serious lung diseases, such as throat and lung cancer, emphysema, heart disease, circulatory problems, and a myriad of other cancers. Smoking cigarettes prematurely ages the faces of smokers. It also affects the vocal cords by irritating, drying, inflaming them and causing them to swell. According to Dr. Ivan Hernandez of Bayview Center For Medical Health Inc. "This leads to improper vocal cord vibration and function. Smoking also may promote acid reflux, which can affect the vocal cords. Finally, smoking degrades lung function, which affects the voice by decreasing airflow through the vocal cords." This is why women smokers sound like men and smoking even changes men's voices as they age.

A cigarette does not help you with your stress. It does not help you cope with your life. You are ingesting a drug and have become dependent and addicted to it. For each puff, you increase your chances of many forms of cancer, along with emphysema and other lung illnesses. As a smoker, when you catch a cold, you will end up with a secondary infection such as bronchitis or an upper respiratory infection.

The biggest illusion with smoking is that you need a cigarette to cope with stress. The truth is you will cope with stress just fine without a cigarette. You do not need tobacco for stress. You want to smoke because you are addicted to the drug nicotine. Each time you take a puff, you are experiencing mini crack hits of chemical releases to your brain. Times the amount of cigarettes, you smoke by 15 puffs. If you are smoking a pack, this equals 300 puffs or crack like hits of chemicals in your brain. This is why cigarette smoking is highly addictive. So much for cigarette smoking as taking up a habit; it is a drug and no different than any other addiction, denial and all.

The denial for cigarette smokers is just as ridiculous sounding as it is for alcoholics. A sinus infection sufferer and a person with asthma both told me that cigarettes had nothing to do with their illnesses or healing from them. Many smokers who develop illnesses related to their habit will tell you their vice is not to blame.

Depressants

One takes barbiturates or benzodiazepines to relax, to feel better about his or her life and less bothered by stress. Alcoholics often chase their drinks with barbs and benzos to boost the effect of alcohol or as a sleep aid. Barbiturates work by depressing (slowing down) the activity of nerves, muscles, heart tissue, and the brain. The negative effects of barbiturate intoxication include lowered blood pressure, fatigue, fever, unusual excitement, irritability, dizziness, poor concentration, sedation, confusion, impaired coordination and judgment, addiction, and respiratory depression and arrest, which may lead to death.

In addition possible effects from using high doses include muscle weakness, skin rashes, weight gain, increased risk of accidents, increased chance of falling, sexual problems, menstrual irregularities, and memory loss. They can also cause confusion and difficulty thinking clearly, lethargy and lack of motivation, fatigue, drowsiness, difficulty sleeping and disturbing dreams, nausea, personality change and changes in emotional responses, anxiety, irritability, paranoia and aggression, and depression.

Benzodiazepines work on GABA, which is the brain's tranquillizing neurotransmitter. Benzos enhance the effect of GABA. Anxiety and panic attacks cause the brain to become over active. This is when the brain's tranquillizing chemicals come into action.

Benzos are the chemical variety of the brain's own compounds. Because of the increase of these chemicals, there is an excessive slowdown of these cells and the brain's tranquilizing transmitters are reduced. These transmitters are responsible for alertness, memory, co-ordination, emotional responses, heart rate, and blood pressure.

The failure to produce enough tranquilizing transmitters affects the functioning of the above-mentioned body systems. Prolonged use of benzodiazepines forces the brain to make physical changes to overcome the effects from the drug. The user then develops a tolerance, which happens because GABA, the natural calming chemical, produced by the brain becomes less effective.

Depressant Withdrawal

When one tries to discontinue benzos after long-term use, the adaptations produced when becoming tolerant to them force the brain to go into over drive. This results in anxiety, memory problems, panic attacks, paranoia, and agoraphobia. A combination of these symptoms is what occurs during withdrawal. Eventually, the brain returns to produce the normal GABA state at which time the withdrawal is complete. The time to get back to natural GABA activity varies from person to person. When one takes a barb or a benzo they want to relax and feel less anxious. The pill adds chemicals to their own body's chemicals and then throws off systems in the entire body. Like with most drugs you need more for the same effect.

Stimulants-Cocaine

One of the greatest illusionary drugs is cocaine. Cocaine increases one's energy, decreases the appetite, raises heart rate and blood pressure, and constricts the blood vessels. It also raises body temperature sometimes into a fever, and dilates pupils, making the user light sensitive. These are the stimulant effects from the drug. Long-term effects of cocaine are addiction, disturbed mood and irritability, violent mood swings, paranoia, restlessness, auditory hallucinations i.e. hearing things, and serious health problems. Cocaine can cause a heart attack, lung failure, or stroke. An overdose of cocaine can lead to an irregular heartbeat of heart failure, high blood pressure resulting in brain hemorrhage, convulsions and respiratory failure.

Cocaine is highly addictive and smoking crack is more habit forming than snorting the drug. The addict is under the impression that cocaine makes them feel wonderful, the best they have ever felt, but all that they are doing is firing off all of their own body's chemicals at once. The user at no time achieves the high they received upon first use. They spend a good deal of time chasing the initial experience that they never get back. Cocaine and crack users develop a tolerance upon use. The euphoric feeling felt the first time, never reoccurs and the high does not last as long.

Injecting cocaine produces euphoria for 15 to 30 minutes while the effects of smoking it lasts only five to ten minutes, causing the user to smoke more to maintain the high. Addicts are under the illusion that cocaine gives them these feelings of bliss. It is their own body chemicals producing their high. When those chemicals deplete from cocaine use, the user experiences a crash that is unlike any other. As intense were their feelings of euphoria come feelings of despair so extreme it is as if they are in hell itself. They experience depression, fatigue, and lack of pleasure, anxiety, irritability, sleepiness and a strong desire for more cocaine. When users quit they experience extreme agitation and suspicion.

Cocaine comes from the coca leaf. Natives will make a tea from the leaves and drink it for its therapeutic benefits or can chew on the leaves. A coca leaf typically contains between 0.1 and 0.9 percent cocaine. Unlike pure cocaine, coca leaves contain a variety of minerals and vitamins. These nutrients chemically reduce the toxic effects of the cocaine contained in the leaf. When a person chews on a leaf, small amounts of cocaine is released into their mouth. The digestive system digests an even smaller amount, and the decomposition of it is very slow. The traditional use of the South American plant and habit of chewing coca leaves did not pose any health problems but rather the users experienced the benefits of the plant.

Drug makers process the leaves by soaking and mashing them into a paste and letting all the liquid evaporate. The paste minus the liquid is 60 to 80 per cent pure. Drug dealers export it in the form of the salt, cocaine hydrochloride. Street dealers mix pure cocaine with baby power, speed and other poisons to stretch it and earn more money.

To boost the effects of cocaine drug dealers developed crack cocaine. To make crack, ordinary cocaine hydrochloride is concentrated by heating the drug in a solution of baking soda until the water evaporates. This type of base-cocaine makes a cracking sound when heated, which gave it the name "crack." Crack vaporizes at a low temperature, and the user inhales it using a crack pipe. The smoke does not inhale easily as it is very hard on the lungs.

As one writer stated, "crack-cocaine delivers an intensity of pleasure completely outside the normal range of human experience. It offers the most wonderful state of consciousness, and the most intense sense of being alive; the user will ever enjoy. (S)he will access heightened states of being whose modes are unknown to chemically-naïve contemporaries. Groping for adequate words, crack-takers sometimes speak of the rush in terms of a "whole-body orgasm… Ultimately, the emotional baseline, and affective analogue of Absolute Zero, characteristic of post-humanity in its hedonically enriched modes of awareness may be greater than anything we can now grasp. It may be higher than the rapturous transports of the most euphoric coke-binge in paleo-human history. In the meantime, a drug, which induces a secular parody of Heaven commonly, leads the user into a biological counterpart of Hell."

Crack has dangerous effects in the body. Even users who have only used crack a few times are at risk for: heart attack, stroke, respiratory problems and severe mental disorders. As crack moves through the bloodstream, it first leaves the user feeling energized, more alert and more sensitive to sight, sound and touch. Heart rate increases, pupils dilate and blood pressure and temperature rise. The user may then start to feel restless, anxious and or irritable. In large amounts, crack can make a person extremely aggressive, paranoid and or delusional. Because of its effects on the heart rate and breathing, crack can cause a heart attack, respiratory failure, strokes or seizures. It can also affect the digestive tract, causing nausea, abdominal pain and loss of appetite.

Alcohol and crack taken together can be deadly. Crack taken with alcohol combines in the liver to produce a chemical called coca-ethylene. This is a toxic and potentially fatal substance that produces a more intense high than crack alone but also raises heart rate and blood pressure more than crack, leading to its potentially deadly results.

Crack users speak of chasing a high that they experienced the first time that they never experience a second time. The insanity of the addict is that they chase a euphoria they only felt upon first use. Physiologically it is impossible to obtain the feeling twice. The high was never a high to begin with but the body firing off large amounts of the body's own dopamine. The crash is the result of the damage done from depleting the body's own resources of its feel good chemicals. After some use the brain depends on the drug to release the chemicals. Normal joys in life are no longer enjoyable. The addict lives for the drug. After long-term use, the body is unable to make these chemicals. The hell felt during the crash thus becomes the daily emotional state.

Methamphetamine

If crack produces a tidal wave of dopamine, Meth delivers a dopamine tsunami in the brain. It is the monster of all amphetamines. Crack spikes the body's dopamine in the 350 range while methamphetamine surges it to 1250. Meth's dopamine causes an initial intense rush of pleasure and then a euphoria that lasts for about 12 hours. Users say it is unlike anything they have ever experienced. However, what goes up very high also crashes on the ground quite hard and so is the crash on meth. Like cocaine, meth can permanently destroy the pleasure centers within the brain. While these centers can heal, the loss of cognitive ability might be permanent. Chronic use leads to psychotic behavior, paranoia, insomnia, anxiety, extreme aggression, delusions, hallucinations, and even death. Users who have quit for more than year still show severe impairment in memory, judgment, and motor coordination similar to those suffering from Parkinson's disease. In addition to affecting cognitive abilities, these changes in brain chemistry can lead to disturbing, even violent behavior.

Meth, like all stimulants, causes the brain to release high doses of adrenaline, the body's "fight or flight" mechanism, inducing anxiety, wakefulness and intensely focused attention, called "tweaking." When users are tweaking, they exhibit hyperactive and obsessive behavior. Some users feel insects crawling under their skin, and they will pick at themselves like there are bugs inside of them. This disorder is known as formication One user experienced the paranoia up to five years after quitting meth.

Meth causes the blood vessels to constrict, cutting off blood flow to all parts of the body. Meth causes significant damage to the body. It destroys tissues and blood vessels, and inhibits the body's ability to repair itself. Acne appears; sores take longer to heal, and the skin ages. Addicts look years and decades older than their natural age. Small sores cover some users, the result of obsessive skin picking brought on by the hallucination of having bugs crawling beneath the skin.

Meth suppresses the appetite. Heavy meth users become gaunt and underweight. They grind their teeth, eat poorly, and do not take care of themselves. The chemicals found in methamphetamine, such as anhydrous ammonia (found in fertilizers), red phosphorus (found on matchboxes) and lithium (found in batteries), when smoked or snorted contribute to the erosion of the tooth's protective enamel coating. Meth's constriction and shrinking of the blood vessels limits the blood supply to the mouth. With repeated shrinkage, the mouth vessels die. Oral Meth use leads to "dry mouth." The drug causes the salivary glands to dry out. Without enough saliva to neutralize the mouth's harsh acids, those acids eat away at the tooth and gums, causing weak spots that are susceptible to cavities. Thus, the mouth's acids erode the tooth enamel, causing cavities. These decay further by behavior common in users on a meth high: a strong desire for sugary foods and drinks, compulsive tooth grinding, and the general neglect of regular brushing and flossing for long periods of time. One user had nothing left but root tips in his mouth after using for only four months. Broken, discolored and rotting teeth called meth mouth is a sign of a meth addict.

Meth heightens the libido and impairs judgment, which can lead to risky sexual behavior. Many users take the drug intravenously, increasing their chances of contracting diseases such as hepatitis B or C and HIV/AIDS. Meth triggers the release of brain chemicals that increase sex drive, such as dopamine and adrenaline, which gives the user a sense of well-being, desirability, and a boost in confidence and stamina.

Meanwhile, these chemicals impair the judgment centers within the brain. "You do things when you're on meth that you would not normally do. Unprotected sex is dangerous for meth users who inject the drug and share needles, which can spread deadly diseases such as hepatitis and HIV. In addition, because the drug increases energy and stamina, users may have sex that is more aggressive for longer periods, increasing the chances of injury and the danger of spreading infection. Meth use in New York City's gay community contributed towards an increase in infections of HIV. Eventually, meth use leads to impotence.

Among meth's many damaging effects in the body, it increases the heart rate, lowers immune function, causes liver damage, convulsions, extreme rise in body temperature and stroke. The drug, which causes the most unbelievable ecstasy for its users, literally destroys their bodies. The euphoria is not a high at all, but a release of all the body's feel-good chemicals, the constriction of all the body's vessels and the ingestion of seriously dangerous chemicals.

Ecstasy

The club drug ecstasy or MDMA is a powerful stimulant with hallucinogenic effects. It releases a mass of serotonin and enhances dopamine, both pleasure chemicals in the brain. Many who use it claim it is one of the most beautiful drugs available because it makes you feel happiness and bliss. These feelings result from the flood of serotonin and dopamine within the brain. Thus, the drug does not add anything to make you feel this good but again fires off your own brain chemicals. It dehydrates you and can cause brain damage with prolonged use. According to one user:

> "Okay, I admit E does make you feel great, BUT it kills you from the inside. I've rolled before, and I've been dizzy and depressed after. E causes serious brain damage. It affects brain cells and they don't go back to normal. It makes you lose your memory, and you won't be able to think. It doesn't help you. Think of it this way: you are turning yourself into a mentally retarded kid. It releases your serotonin, which is what makes you happy, but it makes you even more depressed than you already were because it sucks ALL of the serotonin out of you. ... It affects your emotions, so you can feel worse than heroin or other drugs."

The release of mega amounts of serotonin and dopamine causes the following "bliss" in ecstasy users:

A general and subjective alteration in consciousness
A strong sense of inner peace and self-acceptance
Diminished aggression, hostility, and jealousy
Diminished fear, anxiety, and insecurity
Extreme mood lift with accompanying euphoria
Feelings of empathy, compassion, and forgiveness toward others
Feelings of intimacy and even love for others
The ability to discuss anxiety-provoking topics with ease

FREE FROM CAPTIVITY

Intensified bodily senses (hearing, touch, smell, vision, taste)
Substantial enhancement of the appreciation of music quality
Mild psychedelia: auditory and visual distortions
Stimulation, arousal, and hyperactivity (e.g., many users get an "uncontrollable urge to dance" while under the influence)
Increased energy, endurance and self confidence
Increased alertness, awareness, and wakefulness
Increased desire, drive, and motivation
Analgesia or decreased pain sensitivity

An ecstasy user described the effects as follows:

Visual effects
Colors look different, things are very bright.
If you stare at something for a while, it will morph
Milder than hallucinogens, closed-eyes visuals, like dreams
Spinning glow lights in the dark mesmerize you

Social effects
You feel very intimate, it's like when you love someone
You feel really good about yourself, really accepting and loving
You feel at one with the world and everybody and are nice to everyone.

Physical effects
It feels great to be touched, you crave tactile sensation
Showering feels amazing, your pupils become very large
You feel like you want to suck on things, that is the reason why
Many ravers carry a pacifier or lollipops
You stay active for hours, you are not tired
Your eyes may start moving by themselves, it is called nystagmus, you have an increased appreciation of music.

After effects
You feel depressed during the come down or for a couple days after. This is because your brain has used up all of its serotonin levels and needs to rebuild them. Make sure you get rest and eat well. Take some 5-htp supplements and eat

turkey and bananas. You may have trouble going to sleep, but when you do you will sleep a lot because you used a lot of energy:
You cannot sleep well any more
Terrible nightmares
Constant twitching and have to keep my hands occupied.
Loss of short-term memory
Difficulty in getting the right words out
Can never fully relax
Loss of appetite
This is from experience, NOT from a textbook.

Studies in lab animals have shown that ecstasy can lead to brain damage. Regular use of ecstasy may affect your body's ability to produce serotonin, which results in mood disorders, depression, sexual dysfunction and sleep disorders. The effects of ecstasy depend on the strength, dose, and state of mind of the person taking the drug.

Some of the immediate effects of ecstasy include:
- nausea
- dilated pupils
- loss of appetite
- loss of inhibitions
- risk taking behavior
- feelings of confidence
- increased sexual urges
- sweating and dehydration
- increased body temperature
- sensitivity to light and sound
- jaw clenching/teeth grinding
- increased heart rate and blood pressure.

In the days following ecstasy use, the after effects (come down) commonly include; fatigue, muscle aches, irritability, poor concentration, insomnia, decreased appetite, anxiety and despair. While scientists know little about long-term effects of ecstasy, due to lack of quality research, it is generally believed that frequent use will result in health problems, which result from long-term use. Ongoing effects may include depression, anxiety and psychosis.

Any ecstasy is probably cut with something else; it can be cut with heroin, methamphetamine, ketamine, amphetamines, opiates and LSD.

Extended use of ecstasy causes difficulty differentiating reality and fantasy, and causes problems concentrating. Studies have found that ecstasy destroys certain cells within the brain. While the cells may re-connect after discontinued use of the drug, they do not re-connect normally. Like most drugs, this one impairs memory and can cause paranoia, anxiety, and confusion.

Ecstasy is not the magic pill. It fires off all of your serotonin and some dopamine, and you feel real good because your body's own chemicals are being released. The discharge of large amounts of serotonin causes after effects and side effects that do not make the little pill a happy pill after all.

Marijuana

When Marijuana is smoked or eaten, marijuana triggers a mild euphoria and increased sensitivity to bodily sensations, along with a range of other perceptual distortions. The effects peak within an hour or two and fade altogether in 3-4 hours. After-effects can include a slight hangover and impaired concentration.

Marijuana composes of over 400 chemical components of which 60 cannabinoids exist only in marijuana. THC delta-9 tetrahydrocannabinol, triggers the drugs main actions in the body. It acts upon specific sites within the brain, called cannabinoid receptors, and launches a series of cellular reactions. Some brain areas have many cannabinoid receptors; others have few or none. The highest density of cannabinoid receptors that are found in parts of the brain, influence pleasure, memory, thinking, concentrating, sensory and time perception, and coordinated movement. This explains the "high" users describe who smoke marijuana.

Marijuana intoxication can cause distorted perceptions, impaired coordination, difficulty with thinking and problem solving, and problems with learning and memory. In chronic users, marijuana's adverse impact on learning and memory can last for days or weeks after use of the drug ceases. Someone who smokes marijuana every day may be functioning at a sub-optimal intellectual level all the time. THC stores in fatty tissue for days to weeks and might relate to the negative after-effects of marijuana use. A number of studies have shown an association between chronic marijuana use and increased rates of anxiety, depression, and schizophrenia. The age at first use is an important risk factor and is a marker of increased vulnerability to later problems.

Those who smoke marijuana daily, especially young users risk mental illnesses. Strong evidence links marijuana use to schizophrenia and related mental illnesses. High doses of marijuana can produce an acute psychotic reaction; in addition, use of the drug may trigger the onset or relapse of schizophrenia in vulnerable individuals. Marijuana affects the parts of the brain that control emotions, memory, and judgment. Smoking it weakens short-term memory, and can block information from making it into long-term memory. Marijuana also diminishes problem-solving ability.

Research reveals that marijuana has the potential to cause problems in daily life or make a person's existing problems worse. In one study, heavy marijuana abusers reported that the drug impaired several important measures of life achievement, including physical and mental health, cognitive abilities, social life, and career status. Many studies associate workers' marijuana smoking with increased absences, tardiness, accidents, workers' compensation claims, and job turnover.

The latest treatment data indicate that in 2008, marijuana accounted for 17 percent of admissions to treatment facilities in the United States, second only to opiates among illicit substances. Marijuana admissions were primarily male (74 percent), White (49 percent), and young (30 percent were in the

12-17 age range). Those in treatment for primary marijuana abuse began use at an early age: 56 percent by age 14.

Concerning marijuana and addiction, research suggests that about 9 percent of users become addicted to marijuana; this number increases among those who start young (to about 17 percent) and among daily users (25-50 percent).

Long-term marijuana abusers who quit report withdrawal symptoms, including; irritability, sleeplessness, decreased appetite, anxiety, and drug craving. These symptoms begin within about 1 day following abstinence, peak at 2-3 days, and subside within 1 or 2 weeks following drug cessation.

Marijuana increases the heart rate by 50% and irritates the lungs and respiratory airways when smoked. It contains cancer-causing chemicals known as polycyclic aromatic hydrocarbons. Numerous studies have shown marijuana smoke contains carcinogens and irritates the lungs. In fact, marijuana smoke contains 50-70 percent more carcinogenic hydrocarbons than tobacco smoke. Those who use cannabis inhale more deeply and hold their breath longer than tobacco smokers do, which further increases the lungs' exposure to carcinogenic smoke. Marijuana smokers show deregulated growth of epithelial cells in their lung tissue.

Marijuana smokers develop the same illnesses as tobacco smokers, such as smoker's cough, bronchitis, and increased risk of upper respiratory infections. A study of 450 individuals found that people who smoke marijuana frequently but do not smoke tobacco have more health problems and miss more days of work than nonsmokers due to respiratory illnesses.

In addition, marijuana triggers a short-term drop in the growth and development hormones. It lowers sperm production in males, resulting in fewer normal sperm cells. Marijuana upsets the hormones that control girls', and women's menstrual cycles. Weed disrupts chemicals in the brain that regulate mood, energy, appetite, and attention. It affects learning and memory processes, and can cause forgetfulness and reduced concentration. Cannabis also reduces logical thinking and calculation skills, and can impair a user's ability to perform complex tasks, including driving a car.

There is also some evidence that use during pregnancy could lead to unnecessary problems for a developing fetus, and contribute to miscarriage and stillbirth. That is because THC metabolites freely cross the placenta, where they interact with the growing fetus. Possible effects include lowered birth weight, nervous system changes, and delayed learning.

Like all other highs, marijuana rearranges brain chemicals and causes the effects of being stoned. Despite the negative effects for recreational use, scientists have confirmed that the cannabis plant contains active ingredients with therapeutic potential for relieving pain, controlling nausea, stimulating appetite, and decreasing ocular pressure. Cannabinoid-based medications include synthetic compounds, such as dronabinol (Marinol®) and nabilone (Cesamet®), which are FDA approved, and a new, chemically pure mixture of plant-derived THC and cannabidiol called Sativex®, formulated as a mouth spray and approved in Canada and parts of Europe for the relief of cancer-associated pain and spasticity and neuropathic pain in multiple sclerosis.

Opiates: Heroin

The white powder, heroin, made from poppies, is an extremely strong painkiller. Heroin can appear white, tan or brown because most sellers mix it with other substances to make it less potent, and to earn more money from its sale. Some users, when trying heroin for the first time, will experience vomiting and dizziness. When they overcome the negative experience and feel the effects of heroin, they forget their bad encounter and want more. Large doses of heroin put one to sleep and cause disorientation, along with extreme relaxation. Heroin completely shuts down pain, physical or psychological. When the effects of heroine wear off, the pain becomes extremely intense causing the user to impulsively desire to find more heroin.

Overdoses often occur with heroin. The greatest risk for overdose comes when the user has quit the drug and returns to the habit using the same amount of heroin as previously. Unbeknownst to the user, their body reverted back to needing less of the drug, causing an overdose and death. Heroin combined with other drugs, like alcohol or cocaine, can cause death.

Heroin is a highly addictive opiate. Brain cells become dependent on this drug to the extent that users need it in order to function in their daily life. Heroin makes the user feel euphoria and a rush of pleasure, a warm flushing of the skin, a dry mouth and the feeling of having "heavy" arms and legs. After the initial rush, users will go into an alternately wakeful and drowsy state sometimes called "on the nod." Heroin suppresses the central nervous system and the user experiences "cloudy" mental function or a fog for many hours afterwards. Users will begin to breathe at a slower rate, and their breathing can reach a point of respiratory failure. A heroin addict's sole purpose in life is to have more of the drug that their body is now physically dependent.

Heroin can be snorted, smoked or injected, but the most damage to the body comes from injecting the drug. Large, red streaks on the arms or other areas on the body and black and blues at injection sites are noticeable after several uses. Repeated injecting of the drug leads to collapsed blood veins, gangrene and even amputation of the arms.

Many deaths have occurred after using too large a dose of heroin. They go into a coma, and the respiratory system shuts down. This can also occur if the addict takes a large dose, hoping for a more intense high. Sometimes after injecting the heroin, users lay with the needle still inserted in their arm for long periods of time unable to remove them. Death also occurs when the user chokes to death on his own vomit, since coughing is nearly impossible while using heroin.

Repeated and chronic heroin addicts who fail to use sterile technique or share needles will begin to experience the long-term effects of such practices:

    Infection of the heart lining and valves due to lack of sterile techniques.

Liver disease - approximately 70-80% of new hepatitis C infections in the U.S. each year - are the result of injection drug use, and even sharing snorting straws has been linked to hepatitis transmission.
Kidney disease
Pulmonary complications, which are often infection related.
Skin infections and abscesses, especially among chronic injectors who suffer scarred or collapsed veins.

In addition to the risk of contracting the hepatitis virus, heroin users also have an increased risk of catching human immunodeficiency virus (HIV) and other blood-borne viruses. The most serious health effect of heroin use is the possibility of death due to accidental overdose.

Those who use heroin never know how potent or pure it is until they use it. Heroin is handled and cut with other ingredients by dealers. Drug makers mix heroin with sugar, starch, quinine, and sometimes, strychnine or other poisons, adding other potential dangers. Because of the unknown strength and actual contents of the heroin, they are taking, users are at a great risk of overdose and death.

Heroin is highly addictive. Those who inject, snort or smoke the drug become addicted with repeated use. Over time, heroin users develop a tolerance to the drug requiring them to use increasingly larger amounts to achieve the same feeling they experienced when they began to use. After a while, the tolerance level for the drug rises to the level that heroin use in any amount stops producing the euphoric effect the user once experienced altogether. When this occurs, the addict continues to seek and take the drug just to feel "normal." They become physically dependent on the drug.

Withdrawal

When people addicted to heroin try to stop using they can experience extreme withdrawal symptoms and fall violently ill, feel severe pain with sleeplessness lasting days on end. This makes them turn back to the drug for relief. Some users spend a hundred dollars a day or more for their habit. Heroin addicts will resort to theft or prostitution to pay for their habits. The symptoms can include:

- Extreme craving for the drug
- Restlessness
- Muscle and bone pain
- Vomiting

The most severe heroin withdrawal symptoms peak between 48 and 72 hours after stopping use and can last up until a week.

Essentially heroin works in the nervous system by blocking pain. Opiates are meant for pain relief from serious injury or as an aid during surgical procedures. They are not meant for long-term use as injuries heal and are short term. They were never meant to help one deal with mental pain, that is the role of our heavenly father and of the Lord Jesus Christ. He is the great physician who heals all of our spiritual woes.

Hallucinogenic Drugs-Psychedelics

Hallucinogenic drugs cause both physical and psychological effects on humans. The physical effects of these drugs include dilated pupils, elevated body temperature, increased heart rate and blood pressure, appetite loss, sleeplessness, tremors, headaches, nausea, sweating, heart palpitations, blurring of vision, memory loss, trembling, and itching.

A user of hallucinogenic drugs will also experience a number of psychological alterations in the brain. These drugs may cause hallucinations and illusions as well, as the amplification of sense, and the alterations of thinking and self-awareness. It is quite possible to have a terrible reaction to hallucinogenic drugs. Drug users refer to this as a "bad trip" and may cause panic, confusion, suspicion, anxiety, and loss of control. The long-term effects of these drugs can be quite dangerous. These may include flashbacks, mood swings, impaired thinking, and unexpected outbursts of violence and eventually depression that may lead to death or suicide.

The effects that hallucinogenic drugs have on the brain are quite complicated. Many users have experienced whole personality changes. Users claim to have "seen sounds" or "hear colors." Using hallucinogenic drugs, one can induce temporary symptoms of psychosis.

Because of the great interest in hallucinogens, many years of research have been done to try to determine exactly how these drugs affect the brain. Scientists have tried to determine how specifically hallucinogens act. This has been difficult to determine. While scientists still are unable to answer all questions about hallucinogenic drugs, they have been able to determine certain areas of the brain that these drugs act upon.

Hallucinogenic drugs structurally resemble serotonin. (5-HT) Serotonin resides in specific neurons within the brain that mediate chemical neurotransmission. Neurons containing serotonin exist in the brain stem section of the brain. Axons of serotonergic neurons project to almost every part of the brain, affecting and communicating with all of its sections. Serotonin also acts at many receptor areas of neurons. Serotonin is a neurotransmitter, which passes signals from one nerve cell to another in order to relay messages to the brain. Serotonin is not the only neurotransmitter, but it is especially important because it regulates many of the others.

Hallucinogens disrupt the normal interaction between nerve cells and neurotransmitters within the brain. This causes the sight, smell, sound, and feel of things to distort. Rapid mood swings are common, with users laughing for no reason, and becoming terrified the next moment. Someone who has taken a hallucinogen may feel a heightened awareness of all kinds of things, and senses may become confused.

Hallucinogenic drugs are structurally similar to serotonin; hallucinogens have some kind of effect on serotonin. They cause an increase in the level of brain serotonin, and inhibit the rapid firing of neurons containing serotonin.

The effects of hallucinogenic drugs result from the effects they have on the post-synaptic activity of serotonergic neurons. Hallucinogenic drugs directly affect the serotonin receptors (specifically the serotonin receptor subtype, 5-HT2), which is what eventually results in a complex pattern of action potentials and activity.

Hallucinations and other effects of hallucinogens are however very complicated experiences. They are not simply a part of a cause and effect system in the brain, where hallucinogenic drugs act on serotonin and cause hallucinations. Instead, they act initially on the serotonin system, which sends into motion, a pattern of complex action potentials and activity. Other neurotransmitters may be involved in these activities as well. Scientists continue to do research to determine the exact effects that hallucinogens have on the serotonin receptors and to answer any questions that they cannot yet answer.

While some people use LSD for the enhanced and vivid sensory experience, it can cause paranoia, confusion, anxiety, and panic attacks. Like ecstasy, the user often blurs reality and fantasy, and has a distorted view of time and distance. As with other drugs, the hallucinogens do not go into the body and provide a high but rather alter the serotonin in the brain which causes the hallucinations and distorted perceptions.

Mescaline

Peyote buttons taste very bitter. The human body's first response to them is intense stomach pain, nausea, and vomiting. Thirty to sixty minutes, after one eats the buttons, the hallucinogenic effects begin and can last for as long as ten to twelve hours. Mescaline, like amphetamines, can cause trembling, sweating, dizziness, numbness, high blood pressure, and increased heart rate, loss of appetite, sleeplessness, dilated pupils, and anxiety. Mescaline can cause also cause contractions of the intestines and the uterus, and for this reason should not be taken by pregnant women.

The chemical structure of mescaline like other hallucinogens is similar to serotonin. An overdose of mescaline or peyote is rare, although a low dose of the substance can leave users feeling very ill. It is not addictive but there are severe consequences for using the drug.

When a mescaline trip ends, serotonin activity decreases in the brain. This may lead to a condition called dysphoria, or a general feeling of restlessness, anxiety, and depression. When people use hallucinogens frequently, they develop a tolerance, and need larger doses to get the same effect. This tolerance carries over from one psychedelic drug to another. Thus, a heavy user of mescaline will also have a high tolerance to LSD. The body's level of acceptance for the substance reverts to normal levels, once use stops.

Psychedelic use can potentially lead to two long-term mental-health problems. Hallucinogen-persisting perception disorder (HPPD), more commonly known as flashbacks, is the first. In a flashback, the user enters hallucinogenic states even though he or she has not taken a recent dose of the drug.

Long-term use of hallucinogens can also lead to a condition called persistent or drug-induced psychosis (pronounced sy-KOH-sis), a severe mental disorder that often causes hallucinations and makes it difficult for people to distinguish what is real from what is imagined. This occurs when former users fall into long-lasting states similar to psychosis. They may be severely depressed, experience mood swings, and have distorted visions and other hallucinations. These symptoms can go on for years, and may occur in people who have no previous history of mental illness.

Scientists have studied hallucinogens such as salvia and magic mushrooms for treating depression and drug and alcohol addiction. Essentially hallucinogens are poisons. LSD derives from ergot, a fungus and powerful poison that live on rye. These poisons have the ability to mimic serotonin and cross wire many brain signals.

FREE FROM CAPTIVITY

Inhalants

What is so dangerous about inhalants is that adolescents around age 12 who have no sense of the dangers involved mostly abuse them. They sniff inhalants, such as glue, gasoline, hair spray, and paint thinner. The effect on the brain is almost immediate. While some vapors leave the body quickly, others will remain for a long time. The inhalant vapors destroy the fatty tissues protecting the nerve cells in the brain. This slows down or even stops neural transmissions. Effects of inhalants include diminished ability to learn, remember, and solve problems.

One boy died at first use. When I was a young, teenagers were inhaling Sure deodorant. The thrill from the sudden rush eliminated any thoughts of danger. The substances are very dangerous. Short-term effects include headaches, muscle weakness, server mood swings and violent behavior, slurred speech, numbness, tingling of hands and feet, nausea, hearing loss, visual disturbances, depressed reflexes, stupor, loss of consciousness, fatigue, and lack of coordination, apathy, impaired judgment, dizziness, and lethargy. The long-term effects include, inattentiveness, lack of coordination, irritability and depression, harm to vital organs, liver and kidney damage, hearing loss, limb spasms, bone marrow and central nervous and brain damage. Some die on first use. They call this "sudden sniffing death syndrome." It is associated with abuse of air conditioning coolant, butane, propane, and chemicals found in aerosol products.

SSDS is associated with cardiac arrest. The inhalant causes the heart to beat rapidly and erratically, resulting in cardiac arrest. Some solvents are so dangerous that the fumes alone can enter through the skin into the bloodstream and cause damage. Such is the case with turpentine. Exposure to turpentine can cause liver damage.

Lacquer fumes can make one feel instantly light-headed. On the various cans are warning of the damage to the nervous system and brain via too much exposure. It is tragic that the symptoms that indicate excessive exposure are the very ones sought after by those who chose to abuse inhalants. If this does not show the sad state of mind of an addict, I do not know what does.

PCP

PCP is short for phencyclidine. Its pharmacological nature is commonly referred to as dissociative anesthetic; however, it can possess the properties of a CNS depressant, CNS stimulant, a hallucinogenic, and an analgesic. Developed after WWI as a surgical drug PCP was later found unsafe and shelved until 1957, when Parke-Davis tested it again as an anesthetic and renamed it Sernyl. It was effective, but the side effects were severe hallucinations, jumbled speech, and delirium so P-D discontinued testing in 1965. Still looking for a use for the drug, Parke-Davis renamed it again, this time Sernylan, and marketed it as an animal tranquilizer. PCP does not produce a high, it causes the brain chemistry to alter so much so that the person using the drug can become dangerous. It can effect long term memory and cause speech difficulties. A heavy user will also hear voices and sounds that do not exist after cessation of the drug. Large doses cause heart and lung failure and ruptured blood vessels in the brain.

PCP on the Streets

PCP showed up on the streets of major cities in the 1960s and 1970s, but usage dried up because people realized it was a dangerous drug. The U.S. no longer legally manufactures the drug. Street names include peace pill, angel dust, crystal, and hog. The effects of PCP are unpredictable and can include euphoria, loss of inhibitions, anxiety, disorientation, restlessness, drowsiness, or disorganized thinking. There can also be distorted time, space, and body sensations, feelings of weightlessness, paranoia, and the feeling of disassociation with the environment. The user can experience audial and visual hallucinations as with LSD. In the body, PCP raises the heart rate and blood pressure. It can also cause excess salivation, sweating, numbness, and staggering, slurred speech, fever, and muscle rigidity.

Effects of Toxic Doses

In toxic doses, the user can become hostile and violent, acting in a bizarre or psychotic manner. They may attempt to assault other people, or to harm themselves through self-mutilation or suicide. The person may experience amnesia and become catatonic. In high doses, there may be coma, convulsions, and death. Persons who have received toxic doses must often be restrained and receive tranquilizers to calm them down. Many users report profound after-effects ranging from depression, dissociative states, confusion, paranoia, and feelings of insanity. By some reports, these symptoms can continue for years after the initial experience. PCP sells as a substitute for other drugs, causing panic in unsuspecting users. Even in low doses, PCP produces harmful psychological effects. One dose may produce physical effects that last for months.

PCP is an addictive drug; its use often results in psychological dependence, craving, and compulsive behavior. PCP produces unpleasant psychological effects, and users often become violent or suicidal.

PCP poses particular risks for young people. Even moderate use of the drug can negatively affect the hormones associated with normal growth and development. PCP use also can impede the learning process in teenagers.

High doses of PCP can cause seizures, coma, and even death (often resulting from accidental injury or suicide while under the drug's effects). At high doses, PCP's effects resemble the symptoms associated with schizophrenia, including delusions and paranoia.

Long-term use of PCP can lead to memory loss, difficulty with speech or thought, depression, and weight loss. These problems can persist for up to a year after an individual has stopped using PCP.

Conclusion

While this chapter has covered major drugs, it is not an exhaustive list. If you have read to this point, you have gotten the message that for an addict, they are not really getting high but re-arranging their own brain chemistry. In the case of inhalants, the high felt is nothing more than the damage caused by the poisons. It is a sad place an addict will go to escape their reality. They destroy their body and rearrange their brain chemistry. An addict will take a neurotoxin (alcohol) and poisons to help them to escape.

The Illusion of Non Substance Addictions

For non-drug additions, the illusion is that these things will make you happy. If you are a food addict, you abuse food as if it were a drug. While the damage does not happen as quickly, it happens, nonetheless. The illusion of non- substance vices is that these things will help you escape stress and make you feel better. In the end, all addictions make you feel worse and each brings with them some kind of destruction. All addicts find it near impossible to stop no matter how much they hate what they are doing. This is because all addicts find themselves in the prison house, which we will talk about in the next chapter.

4

THE PRISON HOUSE

Addiction takes all addicts to the same place: prison. The definition of prison is a building to which people are legally committed as a punishment for crimes they have committed or while awaiting trial. When a person goes to prison, their lives are not their own. In the addiction prison house, the addict cannot escape, and they are forced to labor at the grinding wheel. This is the large ancient wheel that people manually pushed around a circle to grind wheat. Every addict finds himself or herself grinding at the wheel, and living the monotony of going around and around with their lives going nowhere, but in circles. They want to stop their addiction, but they are powerless. The enemy takes them prisoner and forces them to grind at the wheel. Just like all prisoners, their lives are filled with grief, despair, sadness and the hope for a miracle out of their situation.

What The Bibles Says About Alcohol

Wine in the bible is synonymous with sorrow and grief. While the Bible mentions wine as having health benefits in small amounts; in excessive amounts, it promises to bring grief and sorrow. In Paul's epistle to Timothy in 1Timothy 5:23, he tells Timothy, *"No longer drink only water, but use a little wine for you stomach's sake and your frequent infirmities."* In small amounts, wine has the same effect as aspirin on the body. Drink alcohol to excess and it is a different story.

Proverbs 23: 29-35 describes an alcoholic. It also provides an analogy by describing wine as looking enticing in the glass but in the end biting like a serpent. This accurately describes alcohol's physical, mental and spiritual effects on the drinker. While the snake provides a perfect picture of alcohol's effects, it has another meaning. The Bible represents the Devil as a serpent. Alcohol is the devil's drink and is a weapon in his arsenal. Proverbs 23: 29-35 records:

Who has woe?
Who has sorrow?
Who has complaints?
Who has wounds without cause?
Who has redness of eyes?
Those who linger long after wine,
Those who go in search of mixed wine.
Do not look on the wine when it is red,
When it sparklers around in the cup,
When it swirls around smoothly;
At last it bites like a serpent,
And stings like a viper,
Your eyes will see strange things,
Yes you will be like one who lies down in the midst of the sea,
Or like one who lies at the top of the mast saying;
They have struck me, but I was not hurt;
They have beaten me, but I did not feel it,
When shall I awake that I may seek another drink?

Isaiah 5: 11 warns, *"Woe to those who rise early in the morning that they may follow intoxicating drink; who continue until night, till wine inflames them."* A *"woe"* in the Bible usually signifies extreme troubles, tribulation and a curse. Alcohol addiction is a life of emotional, physical and spiritual pain. In an earlier chapter, we discussed how alcohol causes depression and deep despair; this is what the Bible is talking about.

FREE FROM CAPTIVITY

Addiction is Idolatry

How do we end up in the enemy's hand and the prison to begin with? It begins with idolatry. Yes, addiction is idolatry. The definition of idolatry is:

1. Worship of idols.
2. Extreme admiration, love, or reverence for something or someone: "idolatry of art."

Most people or teenagers begin using alcohol and drugs for different reasons. For teens, it's peer pressure, boredom, rebellion, escape, and lack of self-confidence. For some, alcohol use helps them relieve stress. Others drink to feel more relaxed in social situations. Some drink to pick up their mood or to celebrate.

Notice in the passage in Proverbs is the phrase, *"Those who linger long after wine."* We long for a lover and will search for those we love. We also long for our passions, which can be our idols. It is not the occasional, medicinal or social drink that makes one an idolater, but the person who embraces a substance and seeks it spiritually, emotionally and physically.

Spiritually, because they look to their addiction to fill them, to make them feel whole, better about themselves, to fix their nature or take them away from the problems. In essence they give it their soul.

Emotionally, because they use their addiction to help themselves feel better. If they are depressed, they want to feel happier, and if they are cheerful they want to celebrate with their addiction.

Physically, because they take it into their bodies and use their physical parts to engage in it and pursue it.

In the Bible, God likens idolatry to adultery because one gives themselves to their idol in the same way they give themselves to another person in marriage. God expects us to give ourselves to Him in the identical way we would give ourselves to someone we would marry. Idolatry is spiritual adultery against God because we leave Him for our idols. Addiction has destroyed many a literal marriage because the addict will give him or herself to their pleasure and put it ahead of their spouse and children. This is why addiction destroys relationships and families.

In A Marriage

Spiritually, we look to the other person to help complete us and make us feel whole and help them with their life's up and downs. They help with ours and we join to them from our soul to theirs.

Emotionally, because we give our spouse our heart and our mate is now a source of both joy or pain and both.

Physically, we give our bodies for sexual union.

Our Union With God

Spiritually, we look to Him in all things and give Him our heart and soul.

Emotionally, we give Him our heart and let Him and His blessings become our source of joy and look to him to stay content.

Physically, we honor Him in our bodies and do not use our body for sin but for His purpose, and we present our bodies a sacrifice to Him.

Alcohol and drugs degenerate and destroy a person on all levels:

Spiritually-they become evil as alcohol and drugs cause them to lie, steal, abandon their families, commit crimes, become violent, and immoral, with no regard for anyone but themselves.

Emotionally, as their emotions now deteriorate, and they grow more depressed, angry, and moody, miserable and empty and totally narcissistic.

Physically, their health declines, and are now physically dependent on the vice that they continuously give their bodies over to in a physical union.

The Spiritual aspect of alcoholism and drug abuse is also seen in Ephesians 5:18 in Paul's admonition, *"And do not be drunk with wine, in which is dissipation; but be filed with the Spirit."* Dissipation means squandering of money, energy or resources, other words excess.

Galatians 5:22-23 tells us, *"the fruit of the Spirit is love, joy, peace, longsuffering (patience), kindness, goodness, faithfulness, gentleness, and self-control."* In contrast, Galatians 5:19-21 states, *"Now the works of the flesh are evident, which are adultery, fornication, uncleanness, lewdness, idolatry, sorcery, hatred, contentions, jealousies, outbursts of wrath, selfish ambitions, dissentions, heresies, envies, murders, drunkenness, revelries."* Drunkenness exhibits all the works of the flesh and no works of the spirit. The Bible says in Galatians 5:16, *"Walk in the Spirit, and you shall not fulfill the lust of the flesh."* The desire to abuse alcohol or drugs or engage in any addiction is a lust of the flesh.

Lovers of Pleasure

In addition to the addict being devoid of any spirituality and given over to the lusts of their flesh, the addict is self-indulging and seeks pleasure. In the anatomy of an addict, we said that each addict has a pleasure button that he or she wants to keep on full throttle and not to let go. Addicts are lovers of pleasure and as 2 Timothy states they are, *"lovers of pleasure more than lovers of God."* An addict chooses their vice because they love gratification. Their love of pleasure and desire to feel good keeps them reaching for their idol or substance or drug of choice.

Idolatry

When we think of the idolatry mentioned in the Old Testament, we think of an ancient society that believed in the power of false gods. We pride in having evolved from worshiping statues. This form of god worship exists in tribal communities, third world and in certain modern religions, but it is not widespread like it was in ancient society. However, we have not changed at all. Our gods are many, and they are those things we give our heart and time to. For some it may be various hobbies, for others it can be a person, a technological toy, but for the addict, it is alcohol, drugs, porn, food, gambling, etc.

A characteristic of an idolater is that they give their heart to their belief and will sacrifice their children to their idol. The prophet Jeremiah rebukes the Israelites for offering their children to the god Molech. Molech was the god of the Ammonites. Worshippers of Molech sacrificed their children to Molech by burning them in ritualistic fire. In Leviticus 18:21 God commanded, *"And you shall not let any of your descendants pass through the fire to Molech, nor shall you profane the name of the Lord your God, I am the Lord."* Addicts give up their children to their addiction every day and are no different from the ancient Israelites.

King Solomon erected an altar to Molech; the worship was prevalent during the reigns of two kings of Judah, who partook in the devotion. One of these kings actually sacrificed his own son. Molech had two outstretched arms and an inner belly cavity that was open where a blazing fire burned. A parent would pass their child from their arms into the arms of Molech where the baby would then fall into the flaming belly. Parents gave their children from infancy to age 12 and sacrificed adults as well.

FREE FROM CAPTIVITY

All addicts sacrifice their children to their vice. As horrific as this sounds, all sold out idolaters' sacrifice their children to their idol. There was a story of an Asian couple whose baby starved to death as the parent's addiction to internet war games became more important than caring for their child. This is no different with addicts who have given their hearts and lives to the idol of alcohol and drug abuse.

There exist women who prostitute their own daughters for drugs. I heard from a former crack addict who lived in New York City that the women would give their children as collateral to the drug dealers to obtain more crack. In some third world countries addicts sell their children into slavery to have money for drugs. While these stories sound extreme and most addicts think they cannot relate, when they use they always put the vice first over their children.

How many stories do we read in the news about mothers who go out to party for the night and leave their children alone and because they are by themselves a fatality occurs. Many addicted fathers choose to drink and drug rather than care and provide for their children. They sometimes desert their families totally. Cases I have heard where children's college funds, insurance savings accounts, get sold and used for drugs. Children who will live on corn flakes because mom takes food money and uses it for her vice. While this is not as extreme as selling or deserting the child outright, placing the child second tells them that they are not important, worthwhile or valuable to the parent.

Abandonment is a horrific wound for a child. It makes them feel worthless as human beings because alcohol and drugs are more important than they are. While the child has no concept of the evil power in those substances to take over a person's soul; it was the parent who made the choice. The wounds caused are so great that these children when they grow into adults might abuse drugs to help them deal with their inner pain, and they repeat the pattern. As the children of the ancient Israelites whose parents passed them into the hands of Molech into his burning belly, they will suffer an emotional hell from having passed through the fires of abandonment, which may also lead them to abuse drugs.

Picture of Addiction in The Bible: The Story of Samson

All of our vices take from us our spiritual power and blind us, get us turning the wheel around and around, and our lives go nowhere but in a circle, and we are bound, and blinded and in the prison house. The story of Samson in the book of Judges relays the picture of addiction. Samson was a Nazerite, from his birth, which means that he was born consecrated to God. Samson had God's power in his life and as evidence of this power; he had super human physical strength. With his bare hands, he killed a lion and repeatedly defeated the Philistines, who were great foes in the land of Israel.

When our spiritual strength is strong and our relationship with God is good, we are able to defeat the enemies within our person. Our enemies are our sins we are predisposed to committing; the thinking patterns that keep us in defeat.

Samson: a Love Addict

Samson was an addict, and his pleasure was an area that he put before his God. Samson's addiction was beautiful foreign women. We see this when he told his father in Judges 14:2, *"I have seen a woman in Timnah of the daughters of the Philistines; now, therefore, get her for me as a wife."* While he intended to use this occasion to move against the Philistines, who had dominion over Israel at the time, he eyed this woman.

His father and mother asked him in verse 3, *"Is there no woman among the daughters of your people that you must go and get a wife from the uncircumcised Philistines?"* Samson responded, *"Get her for me; she pleases me well."* Further, along we read in verse 7. *"Then he went down and talked with the woman, and she pleased Samson well."*

Samson was a love addict, and his compulsion was for foreign women. His chose women from the same people who were the enemies in the land of Israel. While Samson defeats the Philistines, who are Israel's foes, he pursues relationships with their daughters. Although Samson triumphs over the Philistines and has some power with God, he has not completely committed himself to his walk with God. He holds onto his vice for beautiful foreign women and gives into the enemy that will defeat him; his addiction.

After this woman, Samson met Delilah and loved her. Delilah became Samson's toxic relationship addiction. Samson was an idolater and a lover of pleasure. He wanted gratification, and he felt good when he united with Delilah. Samson himself said that the first woman pleased him.

Samson is looking to defeat Israel's enemy, but he is attracted to their women. This mirrors our behavior concerning the vices that we do not completely give up. We say to ourselves:

"I will not drink but I will smoke weed."

"I will try to not be promiscuous and will try to curb my sex addiction, but I will still look at pornography. "

"I will only drink socially, have an occasional beer" - which, by the way, never happens for the alcoholic.

I knew a junkie who was clean from heroin and telling everyone he was drug-free and how proud he was of himself, and yet he was abusing cocaine. He believed he was clean because he was not doing heroin. Rationalization comes with addiction. Did it make sense that Samson's life mission was to defeat the Philistines, yet he pursued Philistine women? God commanded the Israelites not to marry foreign wives. When Samson told his father to bring him the Philistine woman, he was disobeying the command of God.

Samson's Spiritual Strength

The Philistines asked Delilah to learn the secret of Samson's strength. Delilah is a picture of addiction. Our vice always takes away our spiritual strength because it destroys our connection with God. If we do not have a relationship with God, it keeps us from ever having one with Him or any kind of Godly walk. Samson's strength lies in his uncut hair. Samson was a Nazarite. This meant that his parents took a special vow and did not give him wine or grape juice from birth and never cut his hair. John the Baptist was a Nazarite. Samson and John the Baptist most likely had hair like Jamaican Rastafarians. The uncut hair was a sign of their consecration to God and a symbol of spiritual strength gained from his consecration to God.

Samson's enemies gave instructions to Delilah. Judges 16:5 records, *"And the lords of the Philistines came up to her and said to her, "Entice him, and find out where his great strength lies, and by what means we may overpower him, that we may bind him to afflict him; and every one of us will give you eleven hundred pieces of silver."* Notice the phrase *"Entice him and find out where his great strength lies."* The addict's vice entices them. The addict can walk away but if the temptation is too great, and they are persuaded enough they will give in to the temptation.

Sampson's enemy next asks, *"and by what means we may overpower him?"* The object, food or substance literally lies in wait as an enemy to overpower every addict. Notice that Samson had strength with God. It is from this power that Samson must be enticed away.

Addictions Bind and Afflict

The Philistine told Delilah, *"Entice him, and find out where his great strength lies, and by what means we may overpower him."* Notice the next part, *"that we may bind him to afflict him."* The vice binds the addict and takes him or her prisoner. While serving in the prison of addiction, the guard's afflict the prisoner. Addiction is never a happy place. A place of bondage and affliction is emotional pain. The Philistines offered Delilah 11 hundred pieces of silver to complete this task. What is significant about the number 11 in this passage is that 11 to Satanists is the number of the Devil. Addiction is the devil's prison house.

Addiction Lies in Wait

As Delilah begins asking Samson where his great strength resides, the Philistines are in the room with her, lying in wait. Vices lie in wait for the addict. If your addiction is alcohol, within the bottle is addiction lying in wait for you to take you bondage. Samson made it easy for his enemy to lurk, he was already in the wrong place and with the wrong person. This is why it is so important for an addict to change people, places and things, because when we are in the enemy's territory and on its grounds, it prepares to ambush us.

Your Vice Wants Your Heart

In Judges 16:6-16 we read that Delilah asked Samson three different times the secret of his strength, and he did not tell her. This is the point in every addict's life when they dabble into their vice, but have not fully given their heart to it. They are still holding on to part of their soul and the things that mean something to them. If they are persons of faith, they are trying to stay close to God. This is when they still hold high their family, loved ones, spousal relationship, jobs, etc.

After the third time she said, *"How can you say, I love you when your heart is not with me?"* All vices want your heart and want you to give it completely to them. This applies for all addictions: alcohol, drugs, sex, food, work, the internet, etc.

At this point, Samson's heart was not fully with Delilah because he knew that loving Delilah was wrong, and against everything that he believed in. Loving her went against the God of Israel's commands.

The Obsession For the Substance

Notice in the next verse, Judges 16:16, *"And it came to pass, when she pestered him daily with her words and pressed him, so that his soul was vexed to death."* This is the story of every addict who begins to dabble into a vice; they become vexed by their addiction. An example is a smoker who tries to quit smoking, but cannot stop because they incessantly think cigarettes. Another instance is the sex addict who has sex on their minds continuously. The alcoholic who battles liquor and now cannot stop thinking about drinking while trying to stay sober.

There was a man who was battling alcohol addiction, and he was back with his family and was trying to stay sober. However, at Thanksgiving while at a family party, there was alcohol, and he gave into temptation. He drank one or two glasses of wine. After that day, the desire to drink plagued him so fiercely that two months later he left his family to go on a binge that was unlike any bender he had been on before. During this spree, he moved to a State that was clear across the country from his family, abandoning them totally. This State he had visited, but was never fond of, and he found himself a place he could go and drink and drug himself to his heart's desire.

For what happened to this man also happened to Sampson, for verse 17 states, *"then he told her all his heart and said to her, "No razor has ever come upon my head, for I have been a Nazarite to God from my mother's womb. If I am shaven then my strength will leave me and I shall become weak, and be like any other man."* In this sentence, Samson not only gave into the temptation but also gave his heart to Delilah completely; just as the man who abandoned his family came to the place where he gave his heart to his vice and left behind all that had mattered to him as a sober person.

Into The Devil's Prison House

When Delilah knew she had Samson's heart, and he told her the truth, she immediately contacted the Philistines. The first thing they did was bring her the money. The exchange of money is significant here because the Scriptures tell the believer that God buys them for a price. Judas betrayed Jesus and sold his soul for 30 pieces of silver. The Devil bought Judas. When you give your heart to your addiction, the devil buys you and the cost is your heart. The moment Sampson gave his heart to his addiction, the Devil finalized the purchase of his spirit.

Idols Have Demonic Spirits

According to the Bible, idols have demonic spirits. These spirits are within the item and help to keep the person bound who pays homage to the idol. A nickname for alcohol is "spirits" and it has a demon over it as does pornography, video, computer games, gambling and all other vices.

God says in Leviticus **17:7**, *They shall no more offer their sacrifices to demons, after whom they have played the harlot. This shall be a statute forever for them throughout their generations.* Notice that God states that these people were offering their sacrifices to demons. God Himself said that demons reside in our idols. The spirit's job is to entice you as the enemies of Sampson enticed him. They want to get you to give your heart to the idol as Sampson gave his.

Addictions Emotional Sleep

After the Philistines paid Delilah, she lulls him to sleep. Delilah was at Sampson's knees when he went to sleep. After one gives their heart to their addiction of choice then comes the sleep, where you do not think, and are not conscious of the real impact of your actions toward yourself or others. In this state, Delilah has a man shave Samson's head. Samson loses all of his spiritual strength because he has abandoned his relationship with God, and all that was dear to him for his addiction. Samson's shaved head is symbolic of his Godly state. Imagine the wild hair of a Sampson, like a lion's mane, now all gone, and he is bald. All spirituality is gone. How powerful he must have looked with his hair and the nakedness of his baldness is the photo of weakness, which is the state of the addict.

Addiction's Torment

From the moment Sampson loses his spirituality and gives his heart to his addiction, notice it reads, *"Then she began to torment him, and his strength left him."* He was now under the anguish for the vice he gave his heart to. In addition, Delilah, who Samson awarded his heart, deceived him, nagged him, used his love for her to her gain, sold him to his enemies, took his strength, mocked him and tormented him. This was some love affair. Samson's love addiction led him into a toxic relationship, which many love addicted relationship's exhibit. Delilah did not really love Samson. Rather she lied to him, betrayed him, mocked him and tormented him. In seeking her, he did not find what his soul longed for or who was truly good for him.

What All Addicts Say After A Relapse

Samson says in verse 20, what every addict says after they relapse or use, *"I will go out as before, at other times, and shake myself free!"* How many addicts have said this, how many times has one rationalized and said; I can stop. I can do this myself. Notice what the end of the verse says, because this statement reveals the moment Samson loses his spiritual strength. *"But he did not know that the Lord had departed from him."* Why did God depart because Samson gave heart to his idolatry? In his sin he lost his spiritual connection with God.

Emotional Blindness

Notice what happens next in verse 21, *"Then the Philistines took him, put out his eyes, and brought him down to Gaza. They bound him with bronze fetters and he became a grinder at the prison."* First, the enemy blinded Samson, because no addict can see that it is his or her actions and their vice that causes their problems. After they blind him, they take him down to Gaza. Yes, alcohol, drugs, whatever your vice, it will bring you to places you would not normally go as Samson ended up in Gaza. It takes you to the dark world of addiction.

Grinding at the Wheel

After the Philistines take Samson to Gaza, they bind him, and he becomes a grinder at the prison, turning the wheat-grinding wheel. Samson, bound in his addiction, turns the wheel and his life goes nowhere but in circles as he grinds. He is now working to keep his vice. All addicts grind the wheel. It is a laborious work for them to make sure they will always have their substance of choice at hand to abuse. They now have given their lives for their drug. They do not enjoy their existence at all. They have found themselves in a prison and forced to mill at the grinding wheel.

Freedom From The House of Bondage

Idolatry brings addicts to this prison. God instructed Moses in the first of the Ten Commandments recorded in Exodus 20:2-3, *"I am the Lord your God who brought you out of the land of Egypt, out of the house of bondage."* He issues the first commandment, which Jesus also referred to and said, *"You shall have no other gods before me."* Prior to God issuing the first commandment, He states that He was the one who brought them out of the house of bondage. Indirectly, He is stating they ended up in bondage because of their idolatry. The only way to get true freedom is by turning to God, which is similar to the first three steps of AA:

1. We admitted we were powerless over alcohol—that our lives had become unmanageable.
2. Came to believe that a Power greater than ourselves could restore us to sanity.
3. Made a decision to turn our will and our lives over to the care of God as we understood Him.

What is Your Delilah?

Notice what happened to Sampson after he gave his heart to his vice, which for him was Delilah. Samson was a love addict, but every addict has a Delilah. As addicts, we have to examine our lives and ask: what is our Delilah? For some, it is a particular substance and for others, it can be food, gambling, work, sex, pornography or love. Each addict has their Delilah, and their Delilah can change as they cross into other vices.

A food addict always wants to eat, and they cannot stop. They will shove everything in their mouth until they cannot eat anymore. Food is their obsession. Usually food addicts seek after carbohydrates. This food addict cannot figure out how someone cannot stop drinking alcohol. However, when it comes to food, they cannot stop eating. According to a food addict, I interviewed; she would often go on junk food benders. When this woman worked in a convenience store, she used to go back at 3 a.m. and eat all the junk food to relieve her anxiety. She totaled out her car reaching for a cookie.

While this woman was at a psychiatric hospital, one of the nurses came out and reprimanded her for sneaking in and eating all the pastries that were for the patients. There were 12 pancake size pastries, and she ate all of them. This woman got mad at the nurse because she was in the psychiatric hospital seeking help for her destructive food addiction. What the nurse did not know is that this woman was sneaking into the other patient's rooms looking for candy. This woman would go to doctors and ask why she bloated and why was she gaining so much weight as if it were a mystery.

This woman worked as a house cleaner and a couple of bosses fired her because she would raid their homes and eat all the junk food in their houses. They would ask her what happened to the chocolates, the ice cream and Milano cookies? Right after being hired, they fired her telling her that they no longer needed her. This woman recollects as a child sneaking and stealing the snacks from other kid's lunch boxes, occasionally stealing their sandwich.

A male friend of hers, while driving in his truck, saw her driving and scooping her hand into an ice-cream bucket to fill her mouth. She could not shove it in fast enough; or wait for a spoon. She went to bed dreaming about all the different kinds of cookies she could eat. She fantasized about being in a grocery store and having her way in the junk food isle. When she thought of pancakes, she would think of one as big as the sky, and it was not large enough. She got tremendous anxiety when the grocery stores were closing because she had to go out of town to get food. One day while driving with another food addict, they visited every fast food ice cream and burger restaurant on the strip. Her friend was saying, "hurry up, we have to go before they all close, I am starting my diet tomorrow."

The most shocking story took place while this woman was babysitting small children. Their mom had just baked cupcakes for a party and instructed the children that they were not to eat one. She also told the babysitter to make sure the children did not eat one cupcake because she made the exact number for the kids at the party. Despite the mom's instruction, the woman could not stop herself from eating several of the cupcakes. She threw the wrappers in the toilet.

When mom came home and saw that the someone had eaten the cupcakes, she was quite upset and demanded to know what happened to them. The little boy told her he saw the wrappers in the toilet, and he blamed his youngest sister. Mom started to scold the child and the little girl all flustered said, "I don't remember; I think I ate them." Meanwhile, the woman who ate them felt relief that no one discovered the truth of her addiction to food so severe that it caused her to break rules, defy, and steal. Her food of choice was anything sweet and carbohydrates. These foods release dopamine. As any addict she always wanted more. Her Delilah was food.

As I said earlier, we each have a different Delilah, and most addicts have more than one Delilah. We trade addictions, but the most damaging addictions are the ones to intoxicating substances.

By Turning to God, We Get Spiritual Strength

After Samson became a grinder, his hair started to grow back. Although he was in the depths of his addiction prison, and daily grinding the wheel and suffering pain and torment, when he reached out to God, He heard him. When we turn to God, we begin to get spiritual strength. Often most addicts seek God when they have nowhere else to turn, and God hears them. It is the place we find ourselves when no earthly power can help us. The time when we seek Him with all of our heart.

All Addicts Feel That Their Vice Has Got Them

While Samson is grinding the Philistines rejoice over having captured Samson. Many an addict feels defeat over the fact that the vice has them. They cried out, '*Samson is our enemy.*' Addiction is not your friend, and you are not its friend. Addiction is a conquering enemy that is always after your life. It wants your sobriety, your health, your family. It wants to destroy you and by you gaining spiritual strength, you do not give it any power over your existence.

All Addicts Perform For Their Vice

While the Philistines were partying, they called out Samson to perform for them. Every addict performs for his vice. They act by doing things that they would never do. While under the bondage of addiction, they find themselves partaking in the very deed they once swore, they would at no time be part of. I knew an alcoholic who looked down on addicts who abused crack cocaine. He viewed them as beneath him. When he fell off the wagon after 23 years of sobriety in addition to his alcohol use, he started using crack cocaine. This man was now performing for the enemy of addiction. How many addicts have found themselves using a drug, going to lengths they never thought they would go to? This also includes sex addicts who behave in ways unimagined to have their vice. All addicts perform for the enemy and as they do they are completely aware that this is not who they really are as a person.

Sampson's Bottom

The Philistines stationed Samson between two pillars. A young boy brought him out, and Samson asked him to put him between the pillars that support the temple. Still blinded, as spiritual sight does not return immediately, Samson turned back to God, and rather than performing for the enemy one more time, he destroyed them. Samson had hit his bottom. Everyone was watching while Samson performed. This time Samson in verse 28 called out to the Lord saying, *"O Lord God remember me, I pray. Strengthen me, I pray, just this once, O God that I may with one blow take vengeance on the Philistines for my two eyes."* Along with Samson's addiction blinding him, he lost his two eyes, and they would under no circumstances return. Addiction takes part of our lives from each of us, and we can never get back what it robbed. We can rebuild our lives, but we can never retrieve the years it robbed from us and the full life we missed during those years.

The Power of Prayer

Prayer is powerful. Jeremiah 33:3 states, *Call on Me, and I will answer you and show you great and mighty things, which you do not know.* God answered Samson. He freed him from his vice and gave him his superhuman strength back to push the columns supporting the temple. However, Samson prayed in verse 30, *"Let me die with the Philistines!"* Unfortunately, Sampson's bottom was death as with many addicts. He died with the Philistines, but when he died, he killed more at his death than he had killed during his life. Sampson lost everything. He lost Delilah. He lost his eyes, and his life would never be the same. He was knocked down in his addiction, but his prayer was so heartfelt to God and heard by Him, that he attained more power than at any time in his life. However, it was now too late; his addiction had taken its toll and killed him.

Substances are not an addict's friend. Heroin is not your pal. If you are undergoing surgery, it is a wonderful drug, but recreationally it is not your buddy. Alcohol is not your friend; pornography is not your mate. Cigarettes are not your colleague. Addicts act as if the substances they abuse are their friends when they are their enemies. That big container of ice cream that you will eat in one day is not your helper. If you are an alcoholic, liquor is your enemy. Yes, the very substance that you feel will help you the most will destroy you and seeks to annihilate you.

The Devil's Prison House

The Devil owns the prison house. The spirits that come with the idols of addiction take hold of the one who gives their heart over to them and enslaves them. John 10:10 tells us *"the thief comes to kill steal and destroy."* He is talking about the Devil, and addictions are weapons in his arsenal to destroy the lives of men and women. Remember alcohol and drugs are venom straight from the serpent. The book of Isaiah tells us that the Devil owns the prison house. Isaiah 14 describes God's judgment of \Lucifer. In verse 16 it states: *"Those who see you will gaze at you, And consider you saying: Is this the man who made the earth tremble, Who shook kingdoms, Who made the world as a wilderness and destroyed its cities, Who did not open the house of the prisoners?"*

God Frees One From The House of Bondage

Satan enslaves his prisoners and never releases them. Only God can release those who Satan has enslaved. In Micah 6:4 God says to the Israelites *"It is I who brought you up from the land of Egypt; I redeemed you from the house of bondage."* It is only through the power of God, we can get out of the house of bondage. When the Israelites went into Egypt to escape the famine under Joseph's reign, they forgot the Lord their God and began to worship Egypt's gods. Their idolatry led them into the house of bondage. Finally, Israel's idolatry during the kingdom period in Israel led them into the Babylonian captivity or house of bondage. God told Israel that He redeemed them from the prison house. Literally, He buys them back from Satan, who purchased these persons with their own hearts, they gave to his idols, which his demons rule.

All of our addictions are idolatry. We are not addicts; we are idolaters. Our substance of choice is our idol that we put before God and even our own families. Only God can release those Satan has enslaved, but one must turn to God first.

FREE FROM CAPTIVITY

5

FREEDOM FROM THE PRISON HOUSE

Freedom is the state of being free or at liberty rather than in confinement or under physical restraint. Although addicts live in spiritual and emotional prison, they can obtain freedom once they have made a complete and total change of heart and commit their lives to the Lord Jesus Christ.

A theme throughout the Old Testament is the subject of captivity. During the Israeli kingdom period, the prophets warned the children of Israel of the coming Babylonian captivity if they did not turn from their idolatry. The books of the prophet's record the details of predictions of invading nations defeating Israel, and the nation going into bondage. Their idolatry caused God to turn His face from them and instigated His anger. He then allowed invader nations to take them over. The spiritual counterpart to this is that idolatry takes the idolater captive.

The worship of idols always leads to captivity. The house of bondage is the place where one ends up when they serve idols. This was exactly what happened to Sampson. He ended up in the prison house.

Love The Lord With All of Your Heart and Soul

One obtains freedom from the house of bondage by turning to God with all of their heart. We must repent and surrender our lives to Him. In both NA and AA the first step to sobriety is realizing that one is powerless over their addiction and that a power greater than themselves can restore them to sanity. The Biblical truth goes even further to the heart of freedom. The Bible tells us to love the Lord our God with all of our heart, mind and soul. God intends for us to become one with Him with nothing coming in between our God and us. Too often, the thing or person that becomes our idol imprisons us. For the addict, this prison is darker and more intense than anything they could have imagined concerning its grip in their lives. Ironically, they live in denial, in defense of their idol that is not their friend and that now enslaves them.

The extent that an addict will go to defend their idol or deny their vice boggles one's mind. The lengths they go to hold onto their addiction is even more surprising. Addicts sacrifice their spouses, children, and families. They put themselves in dangerous situations and hangout with degenerates who use them, steal from them and have no love or concern for their person. Addicts lie, steal, and cheat for something that will never bring them happiness and is not their friend. Their idol will keep them in a prison where all they experience is misery and emotional torment. After all of this and more such as overdoses, accidents, arrests, and DUIs they still use as if charged with Eveready batteries. Some will even tell you how much fun they have and how they enjoy their (idols) vices.

Addicts make all kinds of excuses for their vice, but the reality is that they made the choice. The substance is what they gave their heart to, and now they have in their body the physical changes and the emotional and spiritual deterioration that comes with their addiction, i.e., idolatry. However, they can make the choice to repent and experience the freedom that is there for them if they choose it. The beauty of the Bible is that with this change of heart God promises deliverance, which means freedom from our addictions and from the pain, which leads us into those addictions to begin with.

In Ezekiel 14:6 God tells the Israelites, *"Repent and turn away from your idols and turn your faces away from all your abominations."* In **1**

Samuel 7:3 God promises, *"return to the Lord with all your heart, remove the foreign gods from among you and direct your hearts to the Lord and serve Him alone; and He will deliver you."*

Yes, God promises us healing. 2 Chronicles 7:14 states, *"and My people who are called by My name humble themselves and pray and seek My face and turn from their wicked ways, then I will hear from heaven, will forgive their sin and will heal their land."*

Jesus told us the most important command in the Bible, *"...The Lord our God is one Lord; and you shall love the Lord your God with all your heart, and with all your soul, and with your entire mind, and with all your strength"* (Mark 12:29-30). When one seeks God completely with all of their heart and makes changes in their lives evidencing this change, they find deliverance and healing. The choice is ours.

Isaiah 59:1-1-2 states, *"Behold the Lord's hand is not shortened that it cannot save. Nor his ear heavy that it cannot hear, but your iniquities have separated you from your God, and your sins have hidden his face from you."* It is our desire to continue in our sin that keeps us from having all the good things that God has for us.

Isaiah Chapter 61: Jesus Frees The Prisoners

Isaiah Chapter 61 is a prophecy concerning Jesus and one that Jesus quoted to John the Baptist. Herod's daughter requested that John the Baptist be beheaded. When John the Baptist went to prison awaiting his death sentence, he doubted and questioned if the Jesus he met and preached about was the Christ. Jesus sent a messenger to John, and He quoted from first verse of Isaiah 61, which prophesizes about His ministry. Isaiah 61: 1-7 is a passage about freedom and healing for the addicted.

"The Spirit of the Lord GOD is upon Me,
Because the LORD has anointed Me
To preach good tidings to the poor;
He has sent Me to heal the brokenhearted,

Jesus confirms His calling and His anointing by God. Filled with God's Spirit, Jesus's ministry is to teach the Gospel to the poor in spirit and the broken-hearted. What addict does not suffer from a broken heart? Addicts are also poor in spirit; they are spiritually bankrupt before God.

To proclaim liberty to the captives,
And the opening of the prison to those who are bound;

Wow, not only does Jesus come to tell the captives about the freedom they can have, but He also opens the prison and lets them out of it. What power Jesus possesses!

To proclaim the acceptable year of the LORD,
And the day of vengeance of our God;

Keep in mind that this passage was prophetic and written before Christ came, but when He appeared, He referred to the passage and identified himself. The *"acceptable year"* was an allusion to the jubilee year (Leviticus 25:10), a time of universal release for people and property, which was held on the Day of Atonement. The acceptable year is the time of the advent of Christ and His ministry and death and resurrection. Jesus read in the synagogue and after the reading, proclaimed, *"Today this scripture is fulfilled in your hearing"* (Luke:4:21). And the day of vengeance of our God refers to His second coming, which completes His mission.

To comfort all who mourn,
To console those who mourn in Zion,
To give them beauty for ashes,
The oil of joy for mourning,

What addict does not mourn for their losses? This passage refers to both mourning a death as well as those losses in life that cause us to grieve. In the Old Testament when someone suffered a death or harm, he or she would wear sackcloth, which made from black goat's hair. This custom is similar to our wearing black at funerals. They also rubbed ashes on themselves. Sackcloth and ashes was a sign of grieving or of repentance.

If someone had sinned before God, a sign of their repentance and sorrow over their actions was to wear sackcloth and ashes. If a person received bad news that turned their world upside down and caused them great stress, they also wore sackcloth and ashes. This was the case of Mordecai in the book of Esther, who was Esther's uncle. When he learned that a decree went out to kill all of the Jews and take their possessions, he *"tore his clothes and put on sackcloth and ashes,"* and went to the midst of the city crying out with a loud and bitter cry. Many of the Jews, learning of the decree, were fasting, weeping and wailing and lay in sackcloth and ashes (Esther 4:1-3).

If the sackcloth was not enough to display to the world that they were morning, the ashes certainly did and they gave one a very unattractive appearance. Jesus said that He will give beauty for ashes. Ashes symbolized what had once been. After a fire destroys, ashes are what remain. Addiction is a destroyer on many levels; it sets fire to one's life. Jesus stated that He will give beauty for ashes.

The person in mourning or distress put the ashes on their head. In beauty for ashes, the word for beauty in the original Hebrew means an ornament, a tiara, a turban of priests of a bridegroom of women. Jesus can take that which we mourn over represented by the ashes and turn it into a beautiful headdress. In other words, our lemons can be made into lemonade, but this is talking about much more serious loss than the bitter lemons that life sometimes deals us. The verse adds, *"The oil of joy for mourning."* Oil in the Bible symbolizes anointing, beauty, healing, and light. The verse specifies the oil of joy. Joy is great pleasure and happiness.

The garment of praise for the spirit of heaviness;

Addicts can certainly relate to the spirit of heaviness, in other words, unhappiness, sadness, and depression. God takes the spirit of heaviness which one wears like a coat and gives them a garment of praise. They are so happy that they can only thank and praise Jesus for what He has now given to them.

That they may be called trees of righteousness,
The planting of the LORD, that He may be glorified."

Jesus calls us trees of righteousness after we lived lives of sin and debauchery via addiction. What a transformation! The planting of the Lord means that this person is the Lord's who he will help grow, nurture and water. To go from being poor in spirit and wearing sackcloth and ashes to becoming a planting of the Lord shows our value to Him, while we feel that we have no value.

And they shall rebuild the old ruins,
They shall raise up the former desolations,
And they shall repair the ruined cities,
The desolations of many generations.

All addicts lives end in ruins, with many desolations. The word for desolations indicates the silence left in those areas of our lives that we destroyed. Jesus tells us that they shall rise up these ruins along with former desolations. The areas of the addict's life that they destroyed while using, God rebuilds and restores. *"The restoration of many generations"* indicates a life of addiction that went on for a good number of years and was handed down from generations. Maybe the desolations ran down from family member to family member, but now it stops with you.

Strangers shall stand and feed your flocks,
And the sons of the foreigner
Shall be your plowmen and your vinedressers.
But you shall be named the priests of the LORD,
They shall call you the servants of our God.

FREE FROM CAPTIVITY

You shall eat the riches of the Gentiles,
And in their glory you shall boast.

The former addict now enters a time of plenty. They own flocks, crops, and vineyards. These represented wealth in Bible times. Their lives now prosper. Whereas the addict was poor in spirit, he or she is now rich. The person also serves God.

Instead of your shame you shall have double honor,
And instead of confusion they shall rejoice in their portion.
Therefore, in their land they shall possess double;
Everlasting joy shall be theirs.

What addict does not come out of addiction feeling shame, and instead of discrace, Jesus provides double honor. In place of confusion, rejoicing. Spiritually we will possess double from everyone else and everlasting joy. What a promise. God takes the addict's shortcomings and uses them to become their blessings. A person who is freed from addiction can help others, and has a better understanding of people. When they are turned around from an addictive state they have so much to offer.

The final verses of the chapter speak of the righteousness we now have in Christ and of God's covenant with those who seek Him.

For I, the LORD, love justice;
I hate robbery for burnt offering;
I will direct their work in truth,
And will make with them an everlasting covenant.
Their descendants shall be known among the Gentiles,
And their offspring among the people.
All who see them shall acknowledge them,
That they are the posterity whom the LORD has blessed."
I will greatly rejoice in the LORD,
My soul shall be joyful in my God;
For He has clothed me with the garments of salvation,
He has covered me with the robe of righteousness,

As a bridegroom decks himself with ornaments,
And as a bride adorns herself with her jewels.
For as the earth brings forth its bud,
As the garden causes the things that are sown in it to spring forth,
So the Lord GOD will cause righteousness and praise to spring forth before all the nations.

HOW DO WE GET FREE FROM THE PRISON?

First By Seeking God and His Son

God wants us to know His Son because in Him we can have the freedom and peace our soul seeks. Jesus also offers eternal life. We can know for sure where we will go when we die. When you know that heaven is your home, this earth does not have the same meaning. God's gift of fellowship and eternal life with Christ is simple to obtain, but few will take it. It starts with wanting to know His Son and believing in what He did on the cross, that he died for you.

All men are sinners. Sin is anything that we say or do that does not bring glory to God. God is righteous, and the slightest sin within us makes us unrighteous in His sight. There is nothing in and of ourselves that we can do to obtain God's favor. Isaiah 64:6 states: *"And all our righteousness are like filthy rags."* God will not even accept one into heaven for his good works. Salvation is by faith alone. Ephesians 2:8-9 tells us: *"For by grace you have been saved through faith; and that not of yourselves: it is the gift of God: not of works lest anyone should boast."* All one has to do is believe that Jesus died for them personally and call upon His name.

But Romans 10:13 promises, *"For whoever calls upon the name of the Lord shall be saved."* God promises eternal life to anyone who accepts Jesus Christ as his personal savior.

John 5:24 states: *"Most assuredly, I say to you, He who hears My word, and believes in him who sent me, has everlasting life, and shall not come into judgment; but has passed from death into life."*

FREE FROM CAPTIVITY

If you want to be sure that you are saved and that heaven will be your home, pray this simple sinner's prayer and mean it with all of your heart. "Oh God, be merciful to me as a sinner, I believe that Jesus died for my sins, and trust Jesus as my Lord and Savior and thank you Lord Jesus for saving me."

He that believes in the Son has everlasting life: and he who does not believe the Son shall not see life; but the wrath of God abides on him. (John 3:36)

How To Draw Close To God

1. Meditate on God, who He is, His Words, and His Person.

2. Read the Bible once to twice a daily. A simple schedule is to start at Genesis and turn a page a day. If you miss a day, it is easy to start where you left off and this way you can read the entire Bible. If you see passages you do not understand, do a Google search and research them. The Bible is the living Word. It is powerful, cleansing, and will teach you about the things of God.

3. Place your love for God and Jesus Christ above all else in this life: family, friends, and life itself. What are the things that come before your love for God?

Dying To Ourselves

4. We must die to self and to this life. Paul the apostle talks about dying to self. Revelation 12:11 tells us of the martyrs during the Tribulation and it says of them, *"and they overcame him by the blood of the lamb and by the word of their testimony and they loved not their lives unto death."* The problem with many of us is that we love our lives too much. Addicts go from selfishness to pure narcissism. It's all about them and in their world its used and be

used. There is no genuine giving or love left within them as they live for their addiction.

5. Matthew 10:39 states, *"He who finds his life will lose it, and he who loses his life for my sake will find it."* When we seek to please the god of ourselves, we actually lose our life, but when we live to please God and Jesus, we live life to the fullest. Matthew 16:24 reads: *"Then said Jesus unto his disciples, If any man will come after me, let him deny himself, and take up his cross, and follow me."* If we follow Jesus we leave all behind. Putting God first means being willing to abandon everything that we put before Him.

   In I Kings 19:20-21, God called Elisha to be a prophet and Elijah threw his mantle on him as evidence of God's calling. Elisha was a farmer plowing the field with his oxen. Upon his calling he took the plow and broke it up to use it for a fire and slaughtered the oxen. He held a feast for all of his neighbors who came and ate. The Bible tells us, *"Then he arose and followed Elijah, and became his servant."* Elisha completely destroyed all that pertained to his old life before following God completely.

Most Important Goal Each Day

6. Set knowing God and Jesus Christ as your most important goal each day and place your main focus on Him.

7. If you are not in a church, find a Bible-believing congregation close to you and start attending it on a regular basis. Hearing the preaching and teaching of the Word and fellowship with other believers will strengthen your faith. It will also help you grow in the knowledge of who God is and of His Son Jesus Christ. In church, you will find support and can ask for prayer. Some churches

have groups and program specifically for addicts; attend these if they fit into your schedule.

Turn Your Life Over To God and Seek Him

Freedom from the prison starts with a change of heart and turning our lives over to God and seeking to learn more about Him. This is in line with the first and second step in AA.

The steps for maintaining your new clean and sober life start with turning your life over to God, and learning of Him and His Son. You will learn of Him by attending a good Bible believing church and fellowshipping with other believers. Sobriety is a lifelong process.

Some addicts get deliverance from addiction instantly and for others it is a battle. If you do have instant liberation you will need to deal with the issues that led you to drink.

Think of yourself as an onion and little by little, you peel off a layer only to find yet another layer that comes to the surface. This book intends to help speed you through this process, which leads us to our next chapter.

6

EXODUS FROM HOUSE OF BONDAGE

In the book of Genesis God promises Abraham a land flowing with milk and honey. The land provides a very happy place for Israel, with the richness of milk and sweetness of honey. It is a site where God dwells among his people. Our promised land represents the environment where we find joy, contentment, richness and fullness of life with our God and our Savior.

In Genesis 12:1-3, God first promises Abraham the land, in Genesis 13: 14-17, God lets Abraham view the physical land. In Genesis 15: 18:21, God makes a covenant with Abraham and specifies the land's dimensions. In Genesis 15:13-14, God foretells the Israelites captivity in Egypt. God told Abraham that his descendants would be numerous as the stars in the heavens. In Genesis 17:1-8, God told Abraham that nations and kings will come from him. God's covenant would be an everlasting covenant and the land would be an everlasting possession.

The book of Genesis details the promise and birth of Isaac to Abraham and Sarah along with the birth of Ishmael to Sarah's handmaid Hagar. Isaac married Rebecca who bore twins: Jacob and Esau. Jacob married Leah and Rachel and had twelve sons who became the twelve tribes of Israel. Jacob gave his son Joseph a beautiful coat of many colors. His jealous brothers took his coat, threw him in a pit and sold him as a slave in Egypt.

Joseph ended up in prison and interpreted Pharaoh's dream, which led to his becoming second to Pharaoh. Joseph predicted a severe 7-year famine that was going to strike Egypt and the surrounding nations. His brothers came to him looking for food. Because of the famine, they reunited and moved to Egypt. The brothers meant to harm Joseph but God used their evil deed for good.

After about 400 years the children of Israel were made slaves by a king who did not know Joseph. They made them work hard *"And they made their lives bitter with hard bondage"* (Exodus 1:14). The Bible then tell us, *"The children of Israel groaned because of the bondage and they cried out; and their cry came up to God because of the bondage"* (Exodus. 2:23). In response, God called Moses who Pharaoh's daughter rescued as a baby. Moses mother hid him, when the King of Egypt killed all of the first-born Hebrew boys. God told Moses that He came to deliver the Israelites and bring them to a land of milk and honey (Exodus. 3:8).

The Inhabitants in The Land

In the last chapter, I taught that to break free from addiction we must give our heart to God. Once we seek God and turn to Jesus Christ, He hears our prayers as He heard the Israelites and came to deliver them. Here is what God said to Moses, *"And the Lord said, surely I have seen the oppression of My people who are in Egypt, and heave heard their cry because of their taskmaster, for I know their sorrows"* (Exodus. 3:7). God knows all too well the pain and sorrow that bondage brings and He is there to deliver us. Notice the exact wording in verse 8: *"So I have come down to deliver them out of the hand of the Egyptians, and to bring them up from that land to a good and large land, to a land flowing with milk and honey, to the place of the Canaanites and the Hittites and the Amorites and the Perizzites and the Hivites and he Jebusites."* This verse teaches that while the Promised Land is a place of plenty it has inhabitants and many of these will try to keep the Israelites from claiming the land.

The inhabitants spiritually represent our own shortcomings, sins or any of the self-abasing emotions that lead us to addiction.

For example, our sin of greed will keep us from a close walk with God and thus is an inhabitant within our spiritual person.

Addiction is an inhabitant of our spiritual self that keeps us from possessing the land. Driving out the enemy is difficult because the roots of one's addiction are multi-faceted. Most often addiction begins with a broken spirit or brokenness such as when any trauma occurs. The feelings of worthlessness, despair, loneliness are so strong and deep that the addict seeks his or her vice to act as a balm over the feelings. The substance or compulsive action that an addict will engage in to self-medicate will not satisfy and take away the feelings. It just provides a temporary escape from the negative emotions. The addict usually feels worse afterwards. They become addicted to the pleasure felt in the temporary escape. Despite the remorse, problems, grief and consequences brought on by the vice, the addict cannot stop.

Before we can conquer the inhabitants of our land we must first come to trust God. He reaffirmed his promise to deliver the Israelites in Exodus 6:5-8, *And I have also heard the groaning of the children of Israel whom the Egyptians keep in bondage, and I have remembered my covenant. Therefore, say to the children of Israel: I am the Lord; I will bring you out from under the burden of the Egyptians, I will rescue you from their bondage, and I will redeem you with an outstretched arm and with great judgments.*

Addiction Surges Prior to Ending

When Moses first instructed Pharaoh to let the Israelites go and release them from bondage he responded by increasing their labor. The Egyptians provided the straw for the bricks the slaves used, but now they had to go out and get their own straw and still make the same quota of bricks. If the slaves did not meet the amount, the taskmaster beat the officers.

When Moses went to the Israelites and told them that God will deliver them from their affliction and bondage, they did not listen to him because *"of anguish of spirit and cruel bondage"* (Exodus 6:9). In other words, they felt that their problem was so great that God would not be able to help them. What must be noted here is often when someone begins to prepare their heart to quit a vice or turn from an addictive lifestyle, the devil will work harder to keep you in in bondage. This affects our faith and we do not believe that God can deliver us and free us from our addiction, even though we desire to change.

The Lord hardens Pharaoh's heart so that He can perform miracles for the Israelites to see (Exodus 7:3). God wants us to know that when He frees us from addiction, our deliverance comes from Him.

When I smoked cigarettes, I smoked about two and a half packs a day. I started smoking at about age 13 and became a regular smoker between the ages of 14-15. Everyone said that I would never quit because they saw me as a career nicotine junkie. I developed chronic bronchitis and I knew that cigarettes were affecting my health. I also recognized that my cigarettes did not please God. I walked the walk of shame every time I went to church smelling of cigarettes, but I could not quit no matter how much I tried. Each time I made a serious attempt to finish my habit, I indulged more than even. I chain huffed with greater ferocity with endeavor. This happened to me with other vices. As I neared my end date, the struggle grew more difficult.

This happened with cigarettes until I got asthma, which brought on symptoms that really scared me. I had no choice but to quit. The asthma frightened me enough to give them up. During this time, I prayed and asked God to take my cigarettes.

I was not sure if I could quit, but the day that I made my end date I woke up with literally a fire in my throat. My throat burned in pain from some allergens that were in the air and I severely reacted to them. It made my quit day so much easier because I could not smoke if I wanted to with my throat burning as severely as it burned. Once I got through my first day, it was easier from that day forward. After I gave up smoking, my asthma went away and I never experienced another burning throat from allergies. I thanked God for the asthma and my inflamed throat because He knew what it took to get me to quit.

FREE FROM CAPTIVITY

Plagues Come With Idolatry

In the book of Exodus, the miracles that God used to get Pharaoh to release the Israelites were plagues, which He directed against the gods of the Egyptians. This included the killing of the first born of both man and beast. Several of their gods protected man and beast and the Egyptians considered Pharaoh and his son gods. When God took the life of Pharaoh's son and the first born of man and animal in Egypt, it was the equivalent of a strike in bowling, he brought down all of their god's at once.

Many people in AA talk about their bottoms and the events that happened that led them to their recovery. While the plagues were awesome miracles performed by God, they showed the worthlessness of Egypt's gods. We worship the god of our vice and suffer from the plagues that show us the worthlessness of our god. Those who worship the god of alcohol will experience the afflictions that come with that god such as DUIs, arrests, loss of relationships, etc. In the case of my cigarette smoking, I suffered the scourge of asthma and a throat that was on fire. The list goes on and on for each addiction, i.e. god. From these few examples, you get the picture and those of you suffering from addiction can relate.

Biggest Trials Come in Our Early Days of Freedom

Pharaoh finally lets the Israelites go, God leads them through the wilderness, and while they were in the wilderness they saw Pharaoh and his chariots pursuing them. Even worse they are coming to water and they are trapped. This is their first trial and their response was, *"Then they said to Moses, because there were no graves in Egypt, have you taken us away to die in the wilderness? Why have you so dealt with us to bring us out of Egypt? Is this not the word that we told you in Egypt, saying, "Let us alone that we may serve the Egyptians? For it would have been better for us to serve the Egyptians than that we should die in the wilderness"* (Exodus 14:12**).** Here God performed many miracles to deliver the Israelites and the first major difficulty they encounter they are ready to go back to Egypt and suffer their past bondage than now go through what they are dealing with. This is very typical of an addict in the early days of deliverance.

When Pharaoh pursues the Israelites, his chariots ride in full pursuit. In our first days of sobriety, the biggest trials we deal with are the messes we made during our addiction years. When they surface we must deal with them without substance or without our Delilah and rather than face them we are ready to go back to our lives of bondage. Notice that the Israelites lie trapped with the Red Sea ahead of them and a pursuing army behind them. How many of our life situations have felt like this?

Note what happens next: God divides the Red Sea. He provides a way out when everything looked hopeless. Not only were the children of Israel able to walk through the sea with a wall of water on either side of them, but as they got onto dry land the water covered the pursuing army and destroyed them all. After this miracle, the Israelites believed the Lord and sang him a song of praise. *"The Lord is my strength and my song; he has also become my salvation"* (Exodus 15:2). Later God instructs the Israelites to do what is right in his sight, He stated, *"For I am the Lord who heals you"* (Exodus 15:26). Yes, God heals us from our addictions but we also have to do our part.

We All Suffer Short Term Memory For Godly Miracles

What stands out in the book of Exodus is the grumbling and complaining of the Israelites and how they quickly forgot God's miracles.

When it comes to God all humans, have short-term memory. God could have bestowed the best memory upon you in the world. You might be able to remember things in your childhood and past most have forgotten. You may even have a photographic memory. However, when it comes to the good things that God does in our life, we all suffer short-term memory loss. The Israelites provide a prime example. Here God performed miracle after miracle in Egypt. He parted the Red Sea, but they soon forgot. They became hungry and started to complain. While following the Lord many of us feel famished. Maybe we are hungry for a job, for God to repair a relationship, whatever it is, when God does not answer the prayer immediately, we complain. God would not act fast enough and due to the Israelites spiritual short-term memory loss, they complained repeatedly.

In Numbers 15:39-41, God tells the Israelites that they need to make reminders of His victories in their lives. We talked about spiritual short-term memory. To remedy their spiritual retention, God instructed the Israelites to put special tassels on the corners of their garments with a blue thread. He also told them that their heart and eyes are inclined to follow harlotry, which in the Bible means idolatry. While one is inclined to desire idols or those things we put before God, thinking of Him allows us to stop ourselves if we find we are beginning to drift.

And you shall have a tassel, that you may look upon it and remember all the commandments of the Lord and do them, and that you may not follow the harlotry to which your own heart and your own eyes are inclined. And that you may remember and do all My commandments, and be holy for your God.

I am the Lord your God, who brought you out of the land of Egypt, to be your God: I am the Lord your God. (Numbers 15:39-41)

We Are God's Special Treasure

When the Israelites came to Mount Sinai, God spoke very eloquently to them and said, *"You have seen what I did to the Egyptians, and how I bore you on eagles wings and brought you to Myself "* (Exodus. 19:4). God presents a beautiful picture of how He cares for us and how He brings us to Himself. For the addict who does not feel good about themselves, and does not place value on himself or herself what God states next is even better. *"Now therefore, if you will indeed obey My voice and keep My covenant, then you shall be a special treasure to Me above all people: for all the earth is Mine"* (Exodus 19:5). God views us a treasure. That is right; the God of the universe views you as a prize.

Most addicts feel unloved and their substance abuse is a means to fill a void. God said that you are a *"treasure"*. For those who feel the shame that addiction brings into their lives, God Himself, the creator of the universe tells them that *"you are Mine"*. In the same way men and women who are in love and give their love to each other will tell each other you are mine. Parents also declare this ownership towards their child and will say, "my daughter, my son." That the God of the Universe would say that you are His, shows you the value that you have as a human being.

He adds, *"And you shall be to Me a kingdom of priests and a holy nation. These are the words, which you shall speak to the children of Israel."* A kingdom of priests in the Hebrew means principal officer or chief ruler. The word holy does not mean solemn, pious, or humble as many think. In the Bible the word for holy means, apart and separate. A holy people are those who do not worship idols i.e. the things of this world. They are clean of idolatry and their focus is on God. They are a spiritual people. God wants us separated to Him. This is what holy means in the eyes of God. We are not part of this world but apart from it. All of this is not easy and takes work.

God's Instruction

It was then that God gave Moses the Ten Commandments. Notice the First Commandment. *"You shall have no other gods before me."* Next God gave Moses the Mosaic law. After giving the Israelites the law, God begins to instruct about the land and he says, *"For My Angel will go before you and bring you in to the Amorites and the Hittites and the Perizzites and the Canaanites and the Hivites and the Jebusites and I will cut them off"* (Exodus. 23:23). What God is telling them is that they will encounter enemies in the land He is taking them to, but He will destroy these enemies.

Our spiritual walk is a pilgrimage. We do not get sober and clean and come to know God and overnight we are fixed and all better. Life does not work that way. It is a process. God is instructing on the course. The enemies they will encounter are those very things that led them into bondage to begin with. Notice the next verse, *"You shall not bow down to their gods, nor serve them, nor do according to their works; but you shall utterly overthrow them and completely break down their pillars."* Overthrowing them and breaking down their pillars concerning your addiction (idolatry) means getting rid of all liquor, drugs, cigarettes, pornography, chocolate, ice cream--whatever pertains to your vice. This includes terminating all friendships with those who joined you during your times of sin. It means destroying all paraphernalia, music, books, and statues, anything that was part of your idolatrous, addictive life. This includes places you frequented, even if it means moving.

We Heal Little By Little

Exodus 23:27 states: *I will send my Fear before you, I will cause confusion among all the people to whom you come, and will make all your enemies turn their backs on you. And I will send hornets before you, which shall drive out the Hivite, the Canaanite, and the Hittite from before you."* God will help to rid of our personal enemies and sometimes these can be people who God will cause to turn their backs on us once they see we are no longer using and have become spiritual.

Notice the next verses 29, *"I will not drive them out from before you in one year, lest the land become desolate and the beasts of the field become too numerous for you."* This is powerful because God said that if He eliminates our enemies all at once then we will have to deal with numerous beasts. If we have no emotional problems because we get complete healing, the Devil will throw beasts in our way that will be so numerous it will make our lives impossible. We may never know what this fully means because I do not think we can imagine a life without any emotional baggage. If we were to have such a life, it would create more problems for us.

There was a movie by Adam Sandler called "Click" in which he was able to eliminate his problems via a genie and a television remote. This in turn caused far more problems in his life and he regretted this clicker. Movies have tackled this theme in several pictures of the person who gets their wish and does not think of the myriad of problems that come from having everything that they want. I believe this is what this verse refers to.

Notice what God says in the next verse (30): *Little by little I will drive them out from before you, until you have increased, and you inherit the land.* Thus, is the process of recovery and healing, it is little by little.

Beware of Snares

God continues in Exodus. 23:31-33, *"And I will set your bounds from the Red Sea to the sea. Philistia, and from the desert to the River, for I will deliver the inhabitants of the land into your hand, and you shall drive them out before you. You shall make no covenant with them, nor with their gods. They shall not dwell in your land, lest they make you sin against Me. For if you serve their gods, it will surely be a snare to you."*

In these few verses, God tells the newly delivered Israelites what they can expect. He is going to help them drive out the enemies. In the meantime, He instructs them not to make a covenant with the nation or their gods. This goes back to people and places that we must remove out of our life to ensure your sobriety. He warns that if they serve their gods, they will be a snare to the Israelites. The word for snare in the Hebrew means a trap, a snare, by which wild beasts and birds are caught, i.e. snares of death, a cause of injury. Addicts know this all too well, by making the wrong choices and not saying no to things they know they should say no to.

The Golden Calf-Quick to Go Back to Our Old Ways

God instructed Moses to go to the mountain so that He could give him the Ten Commandments and the law, which included direction on the construction of the ark and altar of incense. God gave Moses the Ten Commandments. When the people saw that Moses was gone a long time they had Aaron make them a golden calf from their jewelry. Not only did the Israelites revert back into their idolatry, but they were also saying that the golden calf was the god that brought them out of the land of

Egypt (Exodus 32:8). They were drinking, dancing and partying around the golden calf. The people asked Aaron to *"make us gods that will go before us."* This is typical of us to look for another way when we think that God has delayed in answering us or is not there. Usually the path we choose is the one that got us into the problem to begin with. As for Moses, the rest of the verse states, *"As for this Moses, the man who brought us up out of the land of Egypt, we do not know what has become of him."* How many of us have felt that we do not know what has become of God when we encounter the obstacles on our path to our Promised Land.

Moses knew that the sin the Israelites committed was a big sin. The Golden Calf did not go over too well with God. They did not just make any god, they made a god of gold, which means that they took all of their money and gave it to make this idol. Moses talks to God and asks Him to forgive the people and He said that if He would not forgive them. Moses then said; *blot me out of your book, which you have written.* He as God was mad. In Exodus 32:23, we learn that their idolatry brought a plague on to themselves, just as the gods of Egypt brought afflictions onto Egypt. With their party came consequences.

Afterwards God instructed Moses to lead the people to the Promised Land. Moses asked God who He will send with him, *"And He said, My Presence will go with you, and I will give you rest"* (Exodus 33:14). Here God tells us directly that we will have His company and His presence will be with us and give us peace. How much more direct can God be about His being with us in difficult times?

Spiritual Housecleaning

In Exodus 34: 12-13 God elaborates on Israel's behavior toward other gods when entering into the Promised Land and admonishes: *"Take heed to yourself, lest you make a covenant with the inhabitants of the land where you are going, lest it be a snare in your midst. But you shall destroy their altars, break their sacred pillars, and cut down their wooden images."* God further states, *"for you shall worship no other god."*

Numbers 33:52-53 elaborates: *"Then you shall drive out all the inhabitants of the land from before you, destroy all of their engraved stones, destroy all of their molded images, and demolish all of their high places. You shall dispossess the inhabitants of the land and dwell in it, for I have given you the land to possess."*

In the book of Acts, they burned their books in the sight of all (Acts 19:18-19). *"And many who had believed came confessing and telling their deeds. Also many of those who had practiced magic brought their books together and burned them in the sight of all. And they counted up the value of them, and it totaled over fifty thousand pieces of silver."*

This verse provides a perfect example of spiritual housecleaning. You will want to destroy everything that has to do with the god you had previously worshiped. You should look through all of your belongings and destroy anything that is part of your old life. This also helps you with staying sober because by cleaning house and physically destroying those things from your addictive past you are making a physical act to match your heart commitment. In addition, you do not know what you brought into your home that might bring in demonic spirits. When they call alcohol spirits, they are not kidding.

In Pentecostal churches, they teach about "soul ties." We form these ties with people we have engaged in sinful behavior with. You want to eliminate these people from your life. They will pull you down faster than you can pull them up. For many who drink, the friends they make while using drugs, engaging in sex addiction, are not real friends at all. In that world its use and be used. While you are with these people, you know that they do not care about you. They are not friends, not real friends, you might like to think they are but deep down you know the truth about these relationships.

When drugs bring people together, the most important thing in the relationship is the drugs. The same applies to alcohol, food, sex or any addiction. All addicts will use and discard you. Some even deep down despise you as they hate themselves and their lifestyle and you are a reminder of what they hate within themselves. You need to break all ties with these persons and even throw out their contact information. When you houseclean you want to make a list of all of the things that you need to destroy and get it of your home. If you are addicted to pornography, you need to do away with all pornography in your house. You also want to rid of porn on the internet along with emails where you may have conversed about those things. Any pictures that might even be a reminder or knick-knacks you must obliterate.

As the Israelites prepared to go into the land God provided a warning if they did not drive out the inhabitants. Number 33:55 states, *"But if you do not drive out the inhabitants of the land from before you, then it shall be that those whom you let remain shall be irritants in your eyes and thorns in your sides, and they shall harass you in the land where you dwell. Moreover, it shall be that I will do to you as I thought to do to them."*

The areas that we do not work on in our lives will cause us grief. God will allow these things to cause us problems. Such as if you have a difficulty with lying and you do not work on that area within yourself, you might find yourself suffering the consequences of your actions. The same applies to anger, envy, etc. For some their sin area might be lying, for others it might be anger or both.

Demons Come With Idols

After these instructions, God gave Moses directions for the building of the tabernacle. Afterwards He gave Moses The Law where God provided the specifics for the animal sacrifices. These rituals foreshadowed the Christ who was to come.

Repeatedly with each sacrifice, we read of the offering by fire, which was a sweet aroma to the Lord. These offerings by fire parallel our prayers and actions in the most difficult times of our life, which reach God as a sweet aroma.

In Leviticus 17:7 God instructs the Israelites, *"They shall no more offer their sacrifices to demons, after whom they have played the harlot…"* Deuteronomy 32:17 reiterates, *"They sacrificed to demons, not to God."*

Notice God mentions that demons preside over the idols. There are demons over alcohol, which is why its misuse ends you in the prison house. Paul elaborates on idolatry and demons in 1 Corinthians 10:19-21:

What am I saying then? That an idol is anything, or what is offered to idols is anything?

Rather, that the things which the Gentiles sacrifice they sacrifice to demons and not to God, and I do not want you to have fellowship with demons.

You cannot drink the cup of the Lord and the cup of demons; you cannot partake of the Lord's Table and the table of demons."

You may read this verse and think that this pertained to ancient times when people made sacrifices to their carved and sculpted gods. The addict makes sacrifices daily to the god of their vice. They give their time, money and all that they have to their god and over these gods are demons. When you are into an addiction, you are serving the Devil.

Newfound Sobriety Comes With Radical Change

The sober and clean spiritual life is about following God in a radically new lifestyle. You must replace everything that had to do with your addictive past. God says in Leviticus 18:3-5:

According to the doings of the land of Egypt, where you dwelt, you shall not do; and according to the doings of the land of Canaan, where I am bringing you, you shall not do; nor shall you walk in their ordinances.

You shall observe My judgments and keep my ordinances to do them, I am the Lord your God.

You shall therefore keep My statutes and My judgments, which if a man does, he shall live by them, I am the Lord.

No more parties, bars, crack houses, casinos, no pornographic websites or lying, cheating or anything that might have had to do with your addiction

FREE FROM CAPTIVITY

Rebuild our Relationships

As we discussed earlier, addicts sacrifice, their family members to the god of their vice just as the Israelites gave their children to Molech. God instructed the Israelites about not giving their children to Molech. He said that he will cut that person off from his people, all those who worship Molech, as well as the person who turns to mediums. God told the Israelites in Leviticus 20:7: *"Consecrate yourselves therefore, and be holy, for I am the Lord your God."*

During your early days of your sobriety or of your giving up your addiction you will need to work on rebuilding the relationships your vices destroyed. All addicts place their addiction ahead of their closest relationships, which greatly damages them. You were not there for the people who needed you the most.

Forgive and Work on Your Resentments

Along with people, places and things that an addict must change, most who are coming off of substances are filled with anger and resentments. Sometimes they are angry at those who they have wronged who have taken action against their behaviors. Leviticus 19:18 states: *"You shall not take vengeance, nor bear any grudge against the children of your people, but you shall love your neighbor as yourself."* This means no vengeance, or resentments and loving your neighbor as yourself. It means putting yourself in their shoes, trying to understand them and not letting anger and hate fester within your soul. For most addicts this is quite difficult because addicts hold resentments.

In summary, God delivered Israel from Pharaoh and led them out of Egypt, in the same way He gives us deliverance to come out of our addiction. Like the Israelites when we are faced with trials we are ready to go right back to the prison house. We have to learn to trust God. We also have to make the necessary changes in our life and change people, places and things as they say in AA. God has taken us out of the iron furnace to be His people. Deuteronomy 4:20 states, *"But the Lord has taken you and brought you out of the iron furnace, out of Egypt, to be His people, an inheritance, as you are this day."*

The first commandment given to Moses reads, *"I am the Lord your God who brought you out of the land of Egypt, out of the house of bondage, You shall have no other gods before Me."* God delivers us from our addiction and brings us out of the house of bondage, the iron furnace, and onto a path united with Him.

7

THE ENEMIES IN THE LAND

Moses died before passing over into the Promised Land. God called Joshua to lead the children of Israel over the Jordan River. The Book of Joshua, which follows the Torah written by Moses, details the victorious military campaigns, which conquered the land that God had promised. The new nation defeated the inhabitants, occupied the territory and divided it into tribal areas.

Joshua is a type of Christ, or a picture of him. His name in the Hebrew actually means Jesus. God told Joshua *"I will be with you, I will not leave you nor forsake you."* During difficult times in our lives, we do not feel God's presence. Yet, God is with us. Jesus stated in Matthew 28: 20, *"And lo, I am with you always, even to the end of the age."* God is with us in our battles. For those of us who have suffered the pain of abandonment from a parent, spouse, friend or family member, these words offer us great comfort. God is the father, spouse, family member, friend who will never leave you.

God first tells Joshua that He is always with him. In Joshua 1:5, God tells him to be strong and very courageous. In Joshua 1:8 God provides Joshua with the key to success. He states, *"This book of the Law shall not depart from your mouth, but you shall meditate on it day and night, that you may observe to do according to all that is written in it. For then will you make your way prosperous, and then you will have good success."* We gain our power by meditating on God's word daily and by doing what He requests in His word.

Jesus summed up the law in the First Commandment, *"Thou shalt love the Lord your God with all of your heart and soul."* If we love God we will keep his commandments, which Jesus actually states in John 14:15. Just meditating on Exodus 20:2 *"I am the Lord your God, who brought you out of the land of Egypt, out of the house of bondage. You shall have no other gods before Me"* is enough to change your life. When you turn to God, God drives out your enemies, i.e. the demons within your person that cause you to sin.

Joshua sent spies to scout out the land and they went to the home of Rahab the Harlot who hid them, *"and she said to the men: 'I know that the Lord has given you the land, that the terror of you has fallen on us, and that all the inhabitants of the land are fainthearted because of you"* (Joshua 2:9).

Whatever is within you as an addict, if you are under demon oppression, which most likely you are, your inhabitants are now afraid. Notice we do not drive out the inhabitants; God drives them out. Joshua 3:10 states, *"And Joshua said, 'By this you shall know that the living God is among you, and that He will without fail drive out from before you the Canaanites, and the Hittites and the Hivites and the Perizzites and the Girgashites, and the Amorites and the Jebusites."*

Victory Against Enemies Behind Walls

The first great victory for Joshua was the collapse of the walls of Jericho, which the Bible states, *"Now Jericho was securely shut up, because of the children of Israel; none went out and none went in"* (Joshua 6:1). How many of us have enemies behind walls that are in hiding? You may have suffered some kind of trauma and do not understand its full effects on your person or why it led you into some of your addictive behaviors until years from now. Some of these walls may have broken down upon your deliverance from addiction. The good news is that God will defeat even our hidden enemies.

Joshua 6:2 states, *"And the Lord said to Joshua: See! I have given Jericho into your hand, its king and the mighty men of valor."* Notice the king and his mighty men. Books on deliverance speak about the commanding demon and his subordinates which inhabit the demonically oppressed. For example with rejection, shame might enter, and an unloving spirit. Rejection is the king and the mighty men are those bad feelings under the king. God instructed the Israelites to march around the city once for six days and on the seventh day to walk around the walls seven times. At the seventh circling, they were to make a long blast with the ram's horn. When the Israelites heard the sound of the trumpet, they were to shout very loud: then the wall of the city will fall down flat. *And the people shall go up to every man straight before him.* (**Joshua 6:5**) The Israelites broke down the walls as they praised God and obeyed Him. Thankfulness, praise and obedience to his Word are keys to spiritual success and deliverance.

The Accursed Thing

There are times when we praise and thank God, obey his Word and yet do not get deliverance. The story of the accursed thing is an illustration of a time when God does not answer our prayers and why things might not be going our way. This often happens when we battle addictions and it occurred to Joshua. After the great victory of the huge city of Jericho, Joshua and his men went to defeat the men at Ai who were only few in number. The Israelites were so confident that they only sent a small army. The men at Ai defeated the Israelites who literally fled from them and *"the hearts of the people melted and became like water."* (Joshua 7:5) They were so few that Joshua did not send his entire army. Feeling the confidence from the battle at Jericho with its highly fortified walls, which came tumbling down, the battle at Ai was a sure win. However, instead of victory, the men of Ai struck down 36 men and they chased them away quite a far distance.

Joshua, the great warrior now felt like we all do when dealing with defeat, He prayed to God and questioned why God even brought them into the Promised Land if they were to be defeated. Notice what Joshua said after tearing off his clothes, falling on his face before God all day long and putting ashes on his head. According to Joshua 7:6-9:

> *Then Joshua tore his clothes, and fell to the earth on his face before the ark of the Lord until evening, he and the elders of Israel; and they put dust on their heads.*
>
> *And Joshua said, Alas, Lord God, why have You brought this people over the Jordan at all—to deliver us into the hand of the Amorites, to destroy us? Oh, that we had been connect, and dwelt on the other side of the Jordan!*
>
> *O Lord, what shall I say when Israel turns its back before its enemies?*
>
> *For the Canaanites and all the inhabitants of the land will hear it, and surround us, and cut off our name from the earth. Then what will You do for Your great name?*

Joshua is in sackcloth and ashes, which signifies total despair. He tells God that maybe they should have stayed on the other side of the Jordan. His short-term memory has kicked in and he already forgot about the great victory over the highly fortified Jericho. He is already thinking of going back to the other place and he accuses God of the defeat. How many times have asked, where are you God, or why did you let this happen? We have all had this conversation with God. Only Joshua, the famed warrior, is now repeating our words. He ups it a notch and cites how Israel ran from the enemy and how all of the inhabitants will hear it and destroy the Israelites.

Joshua knows of God's promise to the nation of Israel. This scenario compares to the words spoken when an addict relapses. Maybe they take up another vice that takes over from the one they just gave up. The Israelites were happy on the other side of the Jordan, reveling in their deliverance and the presence of God. This new enemy seems so great that now they feel it will completely destroy them.

Imagine the scene: Joshua is in great despair, crying and pleading to God and already assuming the worst outcome. In his distressed state of mind the Israelites were defeated and their first instinct is to blame God. This is something God must not be doing in our lives. We just got crushed. Notice what God says. God tells Joshua in verse 10. *"Get up! Why are you lying on your face?"*

In other words, stop carrying on like a child. God flatly told Joshua *"Israel has sinned, and they have also transgressed My covenant which I commanded them. For they have even taken some of the accursed things, and have both stolen and deceived; and they have also put it among their own stuff."*

After God informed Joshua of the accursed thing He instructed the Israelites in Joshua 6:18, *"And you, by all means abstain from the accursed things, let you become accursed when you take of the accursed things, and make the camp of Israel a curse, and trouble it."*

As the story continues, Joshua makes inquiry and a man by the name of Achan took items he was not supposed to take at the conquest of Jericho. God commanded them to destroy everything except the gold and silver, which was to go to the Lord's treasures. Achan took two hundred shekels of silver, a wedge of gold and a Babylonian garment (Joshua 7:21). God told the Israelites that He sanctified the silver, gold, bronze and iron to go into the treasuries of the Lord. Achan stole from God Himself and the Babylonian garment, which he was to leave behind. He took silver and gold that should have been God's He also took the Babylonian garment because it was beautiful.

Most addictions require money. Addicts will take money from their families or from productive things in their lives to pay for their addiction. The garment took Achan right into the culture and world of an evil society that he did not want to part with. This sounds like addictive behavior, stealing, lying and hiding. While Achan helped defeat their enemy, he took something. I believe we all have taken some accursed thing that we hide and will lie about. It could be as seemingly harmless as a phone number, but it is a number to one of our old companions and partner in our sin. The accursed thing weakened Israel to stand up to a lesser enemy. When we keep something from our past lifestyle that should be discarded, it makes us weak because we are still holding onto our sin.

For the addict this object, name, number, friendship means an open door that we do not want to shut. It will keep God's from bestowing His blessing and even keep us from our deliverance.

God adds in Joshua 7:12, *"Therefore the children of Israel could not stand before their enemies, but turned their backs before their enemies, because they have become doomed to destruction, neither will I be with you anymore, unless you destroy the accursed thing from among you.*

This is so important to God that he repeats again in verse 13, *'Get up, sanctify the people and say, Sanctify yourselves for tomorrow because thus says the Lord God of Israel: There is an accursed thing in your midst, O Israel you cannot stand before you enemies until you take away the accursed thing from among you.*

How many of us struggling with addiction hold onto the accursed thing, the friendships, phone numbers, memorabilia that we should destroy when we begin our life anew. We want to stop our vice, but we keep the one thing that acts as a door to going back to our old life. The thought of living without is more than we can bear so we hold on. God does not accept this. He wants us to get rid of everything so that we can find victory. When you battle addiction it is either all or nothing, when you go forward with God, you must leave all from your addictive life behind.

Joshua destroyed Achan and his family along with the accursed thing and the camp was now free from the accursed thing. Joshua obeyed God and also burned all of Achan's belongings(Joshua 7:15). God told Joshua he must remove the accursed person and burn the accursed thing with fire. Notice that Joshua even included all of Achan's belongings. We need to completely get rid of everything that has to do with our addiction, all people, places and things. Yes, your drinking clothes, drugging outfits, and if you were a sex addict the items you wore or saved during your sexual episodes. Any mementos must go out the door. The Israelites could not get the victory while the accursed thing stood in the camp and neither can we.

After Joshua dealt with Achan, God was no longer angry and He told Joshua to go back into Ai and defeat it. Joshua went back into Ai and defeated its people. Joshua went onto have victory after victory and all because he completely dedicated himself to the Lord God. Joshua fought many more battles and won them all, so many in fact that the Bible lists the many kings that Joshua subdued.

God Fights For Us

The Bible tells us in Joshua 23:1 that for a long time God had given rest to Israel from all of their enemies. Joshua followed the Lord wholeheartedly and during this time, the Israelites had a break from their enemies and could enjoy living in their Promised Land. As Joshua grew old, he called for the elders and their leaders and said, *"You have seen all that the Lord your God has done to all these nations because of you, for the Lord your God is He who has fought for you"*(Joshua 23:3). If we follow the Lord God with all of our hearts, He takes over and fights for us.

Our battles become His. Joshua's farewell speech highlights and goes over the principal lesson that is repeated repeatedly in the Old Testament:

For the Lord has driven out from before you great and strong nations: but as for you, no one has been able to stand against you to this day.

One man of you shall chase a thousand, for the Lord your God is He who fights for you, as He promised you.

Therefore take careful heed to yourselves, that you love the Lord your God. Or else, if indeed you do go back, and cling to the remnant among you—and make marriages with them, and go into them and they know you,

Know for certain that the Lord your God will no longer drive out these nations from before you.

But they shall be snares and traps to you, and scourges on your sides and thorns in your eyes, until you perish from this good land which the Lord your God has given you. (Joshua 23: 9-13)

If we love the Lord God with all of our hearts and have no gods before Him, He will personally fight our life's battles for us. The idols we cling to will cause trouble in our lives.

Joshua Warns Against Idolatry

Joshua continued his address by recapping how the Lord God fought for them and delivered them. Joshua also warned them against idolatry. He warned, *"When you have transgressed the covenant of the Lord your God which he commanded you, and have gone and served other gods and bowed down to them, then the anger of the Lord will burn against you, and you shall perish quickly from the good land which he has given you* (Joshua 23: 24-2).

Leviticus 26 devotes an entire chapter to the rewards for obedience and the consequences of disobedience. While obedience yields peace, strength, plenty, rule over our enemies and God's presence, disobedience brings God's judgments. Those judgments include being overrun by our enemies: fear, wasting, want and destruction. God turns from us and does not hear our prayers. Yet God says that for all of our disobedience he will not cast us away, *"When they are in the land of their enemies, I will not cast them away, nor shall I abhor them, to utterly destroy them and break My covenant with them: for I am the Lord their God. But for their sake I will remember the covenant of their ancestors, whom I brought out of the land of Egypt in the sight of the nations, that I might be their God: I am the Lord* (Leviticus 26:44-45).

The Book of Judges

After Joshua's death, begins the Book of Judges. The Book of Judges deals with driving the enemies out of the land. It gives an account of the wars of deliverance beginning with the Israelites' defeat of the Canaanites and ends with the defeat of the Philistines and the death of Samson.

The Book of Judges takes place in Israeli history before Saul became Israel's first King. Prior to Israel's Kingdom Period, judges ruled over the Israelites and led them into their battles. Repeatedly in the book the theme is the same, Israel sins by falling into idolatry, and God delivers them into the hands of their enemies who oppress them. When the Israelites prayed to God for deliverance from their enemies who afflict them, he raised up a judge who would save them from their foe for as long as the judge lived. However, when the judge died, the people returned to ways even more corrupt than the previous generation, following other gods, serving, and worshiping them. They refused to give up their evil practices and stubborn ways. The actual battles present a spiritual lesson.

God promised Israel a land flowing with milk and honey, but they needed to drive out the inhabitants of the land who would not let them possess it. By not following God with all of their heart, He would allow invaders to come and take over the Israelites and they would not enjoy the peace and prosperity God had for them. We each have a Promised Land, which is a place of good things, and blessing given to us by God but the inhabitants keep us from possessing that land. We bring in the enemy by following after sin.

In Joshua, we saw that victory and deliverance comes with living a spiritual life. The book of Judges begins by telling us that the Israelites served God all the rest of the days of the elders who out lived Joshua. But, after all of their generation died, another generation was born after them who did not know the Lord, or the work He did for Israel. Then the children of Israel *"did evil in the sight of the Lord, and served the Baal's."* In God's anger, He delivered them into the hand of plunderers, and sold them to their enemies. In the book of Judges, we see a pattern of Israel's sin into idolatry, God giving them into the hands of their enemies who oppress them so severely they cry out to God and He delivers them from their enemy.

Initially after the death of Joshua, the sons of Israel took over from him and drove out the enemies of the land but they were not as successful. Some of the adversaries dwelt alongside the various tribes. The Amorites forced the children of Dan into the mountains. The enemies in the land gained strength over some of the tribes. Does this sound familiar? Our enemy is right by our side looking to take us over. These are our weak areas that we struggle with. How many of us are in this state? We battle and cannot get the victory and our opponent ends up living alongside our spiritual self and lies in wait.

Idolatry Creeps Back in

Then the Angel of the Lord came up from Gilgal to Bochim and said, *"I led you up from Egypt and brought you to the land of which I swore to your fathers? And I said, I will never break My covenant with you. And you shall make no covenant with the inhabitants of this land; you shall tear down their altars. But you have not obeyed My voice. Why have you done this? Therefore, I also said, I will not drive them out before you; but they shall be thorns in your side, and their gods shall be a snare to you. So it was when the Angel of the Lord spoke these words to all the children of Israel, that the people lifted up their voices and wept."* (Judges 2:1-4) This is familiar, our gods becoming a snare to us, a thorn to our side.

The Scripture on more than one occasion states that the Israelites gods will be a snare to them. Deuteronomy 7:16 states, *"Also you shall destroy all the peoples whom the Lord your God delivers over to you; your eye shall have no pity on them; nor shall you serve their gods, for that will be a snare to you."* When one comes out of addiction, they must completely remove themselves from all people and places and rid their lives of all memorabilia from that lifestyle. But, if they go back and serve their gods, their idolatry will be a snare. The word in the Hebrew for snare signifies snares of death, a noose, a trap that catches wild beasts and birds. It also means bait, a lure. Your idols or vices are a trap that will destroy you and take you captive. There is no good thing in them. Other snares can be emotions that you battle with as an addict: anger, resentment, depression, which spring from an underlying sin.

Unfortunately, for many of us our addictions are a real battle. We might be able to get partial deliverance but not complete and total victory. For example, maybe you conquered alcohol and drug addiction, but are now a relationship or sex addict. Sometimes we fall back or relapse into old addictions. Whatever it is, we return to serving the Baal's in our life.

When we go back, we lose God's blessing and He allows us to go into the hands of our enemy, which Judges 2:14 calls *plunderers*. As Judges states this occurs because, *"They did not cease from their own doings nor from their stubborn way"* (Judges 2:19). Our lives are always plundered by addiction and just like the Israelites in the Book of Judges, we can easily slip back to our old idolatrous ways. The Scripture says it more specifically, *"They did not cease from their own doings or from their stubborn ways."*

God decided to keep some of the enemies in the land to test Israel. The Book of Joshua provides another reason why we do not find total deliverance in some areas, it is because God tests us to see if we will follow His Word. Judges 2:19-23 states:

"Then the anger of the Lord was hot against Israel: and He said. Because this nation has transgressed my covenant which I commanded their fathers, and has not heeded my voice,

I also will no longer drive out before them any of the nations which Joshua left when he died,

So that through them I may test Israel, whether they will keep the ways of the Lord, to walk in them as their fathers kept them or not.

Therefore the Lord left those nations, without driving them out immediately; nor did He deliver them into the hand of Joshua.

In chapter 3 the Scripture repeats that God left these nations to test Israel to see if they would obey the commands of the Lord and Israel not only failed the test but married into the foreign families and served their gods (Judges 3:1-7). This is like us. We not only fail the test but also jump right back into the frying pan of our old sin. God becomes angry at the Israelites and sells them into the hand of an enemy for eight years. This pattern repeats repeatedly.

Finally, God recounts to Israel all of the enemies he has delivered them from and says to Israel in Judges 10:12-14, *"…and you cried out to me and I delivered you out of their hand. Yet you have forsaken Me and served other gods. Therefore, I will deliver you no more. Go and cry out to the gods, which you have chosen; let them deliver you in your time of distress.."*

God does get to a point when he no longer answers our prayer or listens to us because of our continuous idolatry. Times when it seems that God is not answering our petition might be because of our persistent sin. The children of Israel put away their foreign gods, but this did not cause God to listen to them. Eventually God heard their prayer because the Bible tells us in Joshua 10:16..."*and His soul could no longer endure the misery of Israel.*" God in His compassion listened to Israel and will also hear us if we persist in crying out to Him. God then rose up another Judge to deliver them.

How many times in our lives, do we battle with our addictions and give in to them? We feel that God does not hear us. If we give into our idolatry repeatedly, God might not hear us for a time because of our sin.

Sin Keeps us From Obtaining The Promised Land

The battles in Judges present a spiritual lesson. We each have a Promised Land, which is a place of good things, and blessing resulting from our union with God, but the inhabitants keep us from possessing that land. The inhabitants, these also represent our own shortcomings, or sins. For example, if greed consumes us, that will keep us from a close walk with God and thus is an occupant within our spiritual person. Addiction is an enemy of our spiritual self that keeps us from possessing the land. Driving out the enemy is difficult because the roots of one's addiction and sins are multi-faceted.

Idolatry Enslaves

Most often addiction begins with a broken spirit or brokenness such as when any trauma occurs. The feelings of worthlessness, despair, and loneliness are so strong and deep that the addict seeks his or her addiction to escape the mental prison. The addiction acts as a balm over the feelings, but often the substance or addictive action that an addict will use to self-medicate will not satisfy and take away the feelings. The vice provides a temporary escape from them. The addict often feels worse afterward. The addict becomes addicted to the pleasure felt in the temporary escape. Despite the remorse, problems, grief and consequences brought on by the vice, the addict cannot stop.

It is in this area that the addict relies on self instead of on God, but the addict can conquer these areas in his or her life and get the victory. Hosea 3: 11 tells us that *"Harlotry, wine and new wine enslave the heart."* Harlotry in the Bible refers to idol worship, which leads one's heart astray from God. They enslave a person's heart by literally taking the person captive. The idolater loses his heart to his addiction; in other words, he or she loses their soul meaning their being, their essence. There are addicts who leave their children as collateral for drug dealers, who sacrifice their children to their habit. Their idol takes their very essence captive. The person that everyone once knew emotionally and mentally deteriorates under the influence of the drug.

The pattern is always the same, the Israelites would stray from God into idolatry and become a captive. While enslaved to their enemy, they cried out to God, turned to him, and trusted Him to drive the out their enemies.

How To Conquer the Enemies in Your Land

The book after Judges, which is the book of Joshua is about driving the enemy out of the land and victorious living. For this victory we must leave behind our old selves. In line with leaving behind the old self, 2 Corinthians 5:17 states: *"Therefore, if anyone is in Christ, he is a new creation; all things have passed away; behold all things have become new. The Bible says behold all things have become new."* We read about the variety of enemies. The King of Moab was a fat king. We all have some fat king in our lives; there are enemies that are tall and powerful , each oppress us differently, and each of us have unique foes, but they all can be defeated with the help of God. So how do we get rid of the enemies in our land.

1. **Know the enemy**

All addiction has a root cause, that piece of ourselves that we are looking to fill with our vice. The enemies are those lingering monsters within our inner void. To find your nemesis you need to go to your trauma and see what came in. Often fear, worthlessness, and rejection come in with most abuse. Sexual abuse adds inability for intimacy to the list, either from becoming frigid or promiscuous. Promiscuity is not about love and intimacy but about sex addiction. In coming to know the enemy, many people will also have as an enemy the spirit of their abuser. Men who suffered sexual abuse are most likely to violate other boys. Those who lived with violent parents are likely to become violent themselves. Thus, the foe is not only the inner void that the perpetrator causes but also the spirit of the perpetrator themselves.

While a woman who suffered sexual abuse might not abuse other young girls or young men, she will become promiscuous and treat other men as a means for her gratification in the way that her perpetrator used her. The first step in defeating the enemy in our land is to recognize the monsters within your inner void.

The adversaries are not all visible at the same time, just as you discover one, you must now conquer that one and afterwards another rears its monstrous head. The enemies within our person that lead us to our addictions are multi-faceted. There is not one opponent, but usually there are several or many and there are the strong ones and the weaker ones, obvious in your face enemies to those that we do not recognize.

2. Destroy the enemy

Eliminating the enemy is a process because often we can only take them on one at a time. Going back to the trauma and allowing yourself to feel through your feelings that you pushed down, and buried in your addiction is a good first step. Most addicts are unaware that they have these feelings. When they surface, they are quite intense.

This is also where your spirituality comes to aid you. If you are a believer in Jesus Christ, take him with you to this place to be there with you so that in your mind you are not alone. Our enemies rob us of but peace prosperity and spiritual nourishment.

Throughout the rest of the Old Testament, captivity and Israel's idolatry ending in their captivity is a consistent theme. After the book of Judges, starts the book of Samuel and the anointing of the first king of Israel, Saul. Saul defeats the enemies of the land while he follows God but as he sins via idolatry, he too loses his power with God and no longer defeats his foes. He becomes jealous of David and pursues him to kill him.

Next we have David's reign and afterward his son Solomon and the building of the Jewish temple. After Solomon Israel divides into the Northern and Southern Kingdoms. From here, we read the accounts of the good and evil kings, with the evil kings leading the nation into idolatry. The prophets warn of coming captivity by their enemies if they do not turn back to God. The bondage occurred first during the Kingdom Period with the enslavement of Israel by Assyria and then the long prophesied imprisonment of Judah by Babylon.

While the second book of the Bible the Exodus teaches us about Israel's release from the house of bondage, idolatry leads them right back into captivity repeatedly. The message in the Bible is clear concerning the consequences of idolatry and it ultimate leads to bondage. The Scripture also tells how to obtain freedom and victory from the oppression that idolatry leads one to, which we covered in these last few chapters.

8

MORE

If you ask any addict what they want deep within their soul the answer is always more. They can never get enough of their vice. The heroin addict wants more heroin, the cocaine addict wants more cocaine, the alcoholic more alcohol, the sex addict more sex, porn addict more pornography, it's more, more, more. The desire is always for more. Have they ever had enough? No. An addict has an appetite that will not quit for their drugs, substances, and pastimes of choice. Can a shopaholic ever shop enough? Does a food addict ever have enough chocolate, ice cream or cookies? Is a sex addict fulfilled right after their last encounter? No they begin to look for the next one.

All addicts have a bottomless pit that always cries for more, but somehow they feel that they will be satisfied if they can have it one more time. In addition to wanting more, they want the next time bigger and greater than the time before. For those addicted to pornography, they view and view, and eventually they go onto other types of pornography to achieve a better thrill and each time they attempt to increase the excitement. The same for drug addicts, who mix drugs, alcoholics who combine their drinks with pills and other drugs to food addicts who climb the ladder of fattier, sweeter, junkie comfort foods. Likewise, the internet gamer addict can never play enough and gives up all for the pursuit of his or her vice. The workaholic wants more work, more projects, more success. A greedy person, which is another addiction never has enough money.

Someone once told me of someone who gave up sex addiction realizing that their appetite is never going to be satisfied. They encountered their bottomless pit and realized it is at no time fulfilled. The addict is never content but always wants more because they keep trying to fill their inner void or bottomless pit. This emptiness arises from a need that was not met or abuse that left them scared and feeling unloved. The gaping hole, or wound within the addict leaves them looking to fill it with more, more, more.

If the addict really thinks about it, none of their indulgence in their vice will fill or satisfy their needs. They may at times reach a temporary fulfillment when they ate too much and feel stuffed, the moment after sex, while they experience a hangover, etc., and then once again they are in pursuit for more.

The Bible teaches that the soul of man is never satisfied. The driving force of an addict is their desire for more, and it governs all of their activities. It is an obsession to them as they are now a slave to their god.

When it comes to wanting more, an addict must realize:

1. You will never be satisfied.
2. You will never have enough.
3. Even if you bathe in chocolate or alcohol if these are your drugs of choice, you will get sick, have your fill and later want more.

Overcoming The "More Syndrome"

One of the ways of overcoming the more syndromes is to look at where more will get you and for each addiction more takes us different places. As the cliché states all roads lead to Rome, and all addictions lead to death or disaster.

This is the problem with addiction. More never really gives us what we want. Yes, we will get the temporary escape and comfort from our pain, but it is not a genuine salve, a real healing, just as water on a burn does not heal the burn. For some addicts, it is in a state of wanting more that they realized this was not what they wanted that helped them beat their addiction. For example, a man or woman with a sex addiction who has no problem getting beautiful partners will finally realize that this does not satisfy, what they are really looking for is true intimacy with someone who they can love and who loves them. An alcoholic who has all the liquor in the world and the place to drink it will one day ask himself, "What am I doing, I want more from life than this." For some addicts in a state of more, who are in a position to have all they want come to sobriety realizing that there is more to life than having their vice.

I have indulged in so much chocolate in one sitting that at the end of it the chocolate no longer tastes good, or has the same allure. As a matter of fact, I felt jittery and a bit sick but because more kicked in with all of its obsessive-compulsive attributes, I did not stop eating.

There was a day that my life had a domino of difficult circumstances, which made me very depressed and unhappy. After a major feeling sorry for myself episode and ruminating over all the bad circumstances in my life and telling myself if these things had not happened how I would be happy, I realized that I would not be satisfied because I would want more. Some individuals are living with serious life circumstances. There is no greater emotional upset than loss. Widows, parents who have lost children, divorced person who have lost marriages, people who have lost homes, careers, and if they had these things, if these things were never taken their lives would have been much happier. This is true to an extent. They would not have been content because they would have always wanted more of something.

I have heard of cases of perfect marriages that end in divorce because one of the spouses decides they are not satisfied, and they want more. People who have storybook lives, are at the top of their careers, have money, fame, fortune and love and still end up overdosing on drugs. The problem is that these individuals were not satisfied and wanted more. Proverbs 27:20 tells us that

"Hell and destruction are never full: so the eyes of man are never satisfied." Man is never content.

Proverbs 13:15-16 elaborate even further by saying, *"The leech has two daughters give and give, there are three things that are never satisfied, four never say enough. The grave, the barren womb, the earth that is not satisfied with water, and the fire never says enough."*

Proverbs, starts by looking at a leech, which has two daughters that say give me, give me; other words they want more. In many cases, getting more ends most people in death or the destruction of their lives. First, Proverbs mentions a barren womb because for a childless mother who cannot have children, her desire becomes a consuming longing. The earth that is not satisfied with water, is talking about drought. There is nothing more heart-wrenching than a drought-stricken land with burnt shrubbery that cries for rain and parched animals in search of water, which we know the land and animals will cry for more water. Drought is a perfect picture of a person's inner void that leads them to want more of the wrong vices.

Lastly, the final example of more is a fire, which is never satisfied. Fires spread quickly and burn up everything in their path. A fire needs more material to keep it burning and in its path is destruction and so is the picture of more and its disastrous path.

The More Principal of Addiction

Understanding the more principal of addiction will help you recognize and ultimately realize that you will never be satisfied. Enough will not be enough and what you want more of at no time really satisfies. If you are an addict the minute your pleasure button is pushed you want more.

When I was a child, I loved Oreo cookies dipped in milk. Nature's Promise Organics makes an Oreo cookie that is a healthy version of an Oreo. The health nut that I am I figured I could have this cookie. I even dip it in unsweetened soymilk, which tastes like milk to me because I do not drink cow's milk and use it sparingly and occasionally. My healthy Oreos dipped in soymilk tasted identical to when I was a kid dipping my Oreos in milk. It hit my pleasure button; they not only tasted so good but also took me back to a happy time in my childhood and what happened next is not surprising.

For two days, I ate nothing but Nature's promise Oreo cookies dipped in soymilk. I woke up in the morning and had to have them; I even woke up in the middle of the night and had some. They became breakfast, lunch and dinner. I wanted more. By the end of the box they did not taste as good as at first, but I ate them anyway. You can substitute anything here, alcohol, cocaine, or any other vice. When do I run for those cookies, under times of stress because it is during those moments I lose my discipline and am apt to reach for comfort foods. Enough of those cookies and my good health will deteriorate. Under times of stress, what I really need is a decent diet to help my body and mind better deal with the stress. My cookie story is an example of the more principal.

Some of us feel that if we only had that one thing we would be happy. If we had money, if we could find a spouse, or get an improvement on the one we have. If we can only have that house, car, a child, money for school and the list continues. When we finally get to the place where we have what we desire and have worked for, it is not enough we want more.

More With Obsession

An addict's desire for more combined with the obsessive-compulsive part of their anatomy makes staying off of dangerous substances very difficult. When I first attempted to quit smoking, I lived in a place that did not allow smoking, and I thought that this would help me to quit. My desire to smoke cigarettes consumed me. I not only wanted more, but I wanted more obsessively. It was not long before I was smoking as soon as I left where I lived at, and eventually I resumed smoking full-time. Years later when I developed asthma and health problems, this weakened my desire and obsession so that I was ready to quit. I also enacted a successful-quit plan, which helped me from going ever going back to cigarettes.

More for an addict is like the pain of having a baby. When an addict uses afterward he or she suffers the worse pain in the world and when enough time passes the pain is forgotten, and the addict like the young mother is ready to do it all again. When more kicks in, the addict does not remember the pain but the pleasure. The hangover is never remembered, the near-death overdose, the severe depression, the pain and abuse suffered by a love addict, the disappointment and feeling of being used by a sex addict; all that is remembered is the pleasure. For the drug abuser, they remember the initial high, the sex addict recalls the orgasm, the love addict those moments of holding hands, the alcoholic the first few minutes of feeling better before liquor turned on him or her like a snake. Withdrawal can be agony because during times of withdrawal an addict craves more.

The pain of loneliness, sadness, or depression, drives the addict into a preoccupation with more. In part more occurs because of habit. The addict is used to reaching for more, and doing all that is in his or her power to get more. The lifestyle is all the addict knows. When the addict feels bad, the addict reaches for more. Hungry, angry, lonely, bored and tired, is when the addict's defenses are down and leaves them struggling and wanting more.

Obsession For More

The obsession for substance is no different from any preoccupation. The love addict who has broken up with their lover will obsess minute by minute about their former spouse or partner. The painful withdrawal feels so excruciating that the victim contemplates suicide. All the person can talk about is the other person. They cannot hear a word you say, all they want to discuss is the toxic relationship they left and now yearn to have back again. They want more, more of the other person. The person who seldom made them happy, did unthinkable things to hurt them, they want to continue their relationship despite all the negatives. Relationship addiction obsession is worse than drug or alcohol obsession because it never leaves the love addict, not for a moment. It even consumes them in their dreams. The fixation on the other person makes them feel as if they still have them. The thought of their being alone is abysmal, so like Hell itself that it fuels an obsession unlike any other.

Obsessive thinking is a mask that the addict puts on which covers their real emotions. Obsessive-Compulsive Disorder such as counting forks, insane organization is anxiety-related and masks underlying anxiety. It is the same with alcohol, drug and cigarette and all other obsessions. If you obsess about your alcohol, cocaine, crack, meth, lover, sex, work, gambling, or food, you do not have to deal with your real feelings because those feelings are so painful that it is easier to obsess and think about your addiction.

Each obsession for each addictive behavior is difficult to deal with. Alcohol, drugs, nicotine and caffeine all come with cravings. Relationship addiction is more intense because it borders on the human need for companionship.

Sex addiction is powerful because the body's own hormones stimulate and fuel the desire. Food addiction is the most difficult because we all feel hunger and need to eat to survive.

Aside from the human condition, which always wants more and cannot find contentment, the addict wants more out of obsession. The obsession keeps the addict engaged from confronting what is behind their walls (an enemy of the land talked about in an earlier chapter). The sadness, loneliness, feelings of worthlessness are so great; it is easier to focus on the vice than what drives you to the addiction.

The Bottomless Pit-Inner Void

The addict wants more because the addict has a bottomless pit as part of his or her anatomy. This pit drives all obsessive-compulsive behavior, and the addicts desire for more. An addict needs to examine their bottomless pit.

1. Go back to the place that the inner void, the bottomless pit started within your soul.

2. Examine what it is you are trying to fill. Maybe it started with a trauma you experienced. On the other hand, perhaps you are a sensitive person who feels so deeply you felt your way into your own bottomless pit.

We as persons are like an onion with many layers. We uncover one layer and there is another underneath. We can never seem to get to all the layers. Recovery is a process.

What drives you to your vice? At what point in your life was your spirit broken? The Christian teacher Mark DeJesus has an excellent series on the broken spirit, and he is great to listen to in order to help you get to the root of your drive for your addiction and heal your inner void. It helps in the recovery process to go to the root. Mark theorizes that when your spirit is broken through a trauma you allow in various spirits that now influence and drive you. These spirits the Bible calls by name such as rejection, worthlessness, sadness, depression.

The Dark Side of Addiction

There is an entire demonic, spiritual side of addiction. In an earlier chapter, we discussed that the prison the addict finds him or herself in that the Devil operates. To gain entrance to this prison one gives his or her heart. It is when you give your heart back to God that He delivers you from the prison house.

Although God delivers you, you still have the enemies in your land, which are the battles within yourself. These foes can also be various spirits that have attached to you to oppress you along the way. There are different spirits mentioned in the Bible. The first mentioned is the Spirit of God, and the Spirit of the Lord. Along with Holy Spirit and its associated spirits are the various fruits of the Spirit, which characterize God and Jesus Christ. The fruits of the Spirit are love, joy, peace, patience, which we discussed in an earlier chapter. The Demonic spirits on the other hand produce the opposite and can keep an addict bound in their vice.

FREE FROM CAPTIVITY

Spirits Associated with the Holy Spirit

Below is a list of Spirits associated with the Holy Spirit and with Jesus Christ:

Spirit of wisdom (Deuteronomy 34:9) Joshua had this spirit
Spirit of knowledge
Spirit of counsel (Isaiah 11:2)
Spirit of grace and supplications (Zechariah 12:10)
Spirit of truth (John 14:17 John 16:14) in reference to Jesus
Spirit of Jesus Christ (Philippians 1:19)
Spirit of Christ (1 Peter 1:11)
Spirit of His Son (Galatians 4:6)
Spirit of Truth (1 John 4:6)
Spirit of life (Romans 8:2) (in Christ)
Spirit of adoption (Romans 8:5)
Spirit of meekness (1 Corinthians 4:21, Gal 6:1)
Holy Spirit of Promise (Ephesians 1:13)
Spirit of holiness (Romans 1:4)
Spirit of Wisdom and Revelation (Ephesians 1:13)
Spirit of his Mouth (1 Thesolonians 2:8)
Spirit of Grace (Hebrews 10:29)
Spirit of Glory (1 Peter 4:14)
Spirit of Life (Revelation 11:11)
Spirit of Prophecy (Revelation 19:11)
Faithful spirit (Proverbs 11:13)
Eternal spirit (Hebrews 9:14)

Evil Spirits Mentioned in the Bible

Below are all of the evil spirits mentioned in the Bible:

Spirit of Jealousy (Numbers 5:30)
An evil spirit (1 Samuel 16:14 Judges 9:23, Acts 19:16)
    *The evil spirit from God came upon Saul (*1 Sa 18:10)
Evil spirits (Luke 7:21, Luke 8:2, Acts 19:12-13)

Seducing Spirits (1 Titus 4:1)
Spirit of deep sleep (Isaiah 29:10)
Spirit of heaviness (Isaiah 61:3)
Spirit of whoredoms (fornication, adultery, prostitution) (Hosea 4:12, Hosea 5:4)
Spirit of an Unclean devil (Luke 4:33)
Spirit of infirmity (Luke 13:11)
Spirit of divination (Acts 16:16)
Spirit of the world (1 Corinthians 2:14)
Spirit of Fear (2 Timothy 1:7)
Spirit of Antichrist (1 John 4:3
Spirit of Error (1 John 4:6)
A familiar spirit (1 Samuel 28:7) necromancer, one that evokes the dead, God speaks against these individuals who seeks these spirits to cut them off from His people.   (Leviticus 19:31, Leviticus 20:6, Leviticus 20:27, Deuteronomy 18:11, 1 Samuel 28:3, 1 Samuel 28:7, 1 Samuel 28:8, 1 Samuel 28:9, 2 Kings 21;6, 2 Kings 23;24, 1 Chronicles10:13, 2 Chronicles 33:6, Isaiah 8:19, Isaiah 19:3, Isaiah 29:4)
A lying spirit (1 Kings 22:22, 2 Chronicles 18:21-22)
Unclean Spirit (immoral) (Matthew 12:43, Mark 1:26, Mark 5:2, Mark 5:8, Mark 7:25, Luke 8:29 Luke 11:24)
Unclean spirits (Mat 10:1, Mar 1:27, Luke 6:18, Acts 5:16, Acts 8:7)
Unclean spirits like Frogs (Revelation 16:3)
Other spirits more wicked (Matthew 12:45, Mark 3:1, Mark 5:13, Mark 6:7, Luke 4:36)
He taketh seven other spirits more wicked than himself (Luke 11:26)
Dumb spirit (Mark 9:17) could not speak
Foul spirit (Mark 9:25) in conjunction with deaf and dumb spirit, (Revelation 18:2)
Deaf and dumb spirit (Mark 9:25) Jesus cast this one out
The spirits (Luke 10:20),
Spirits of devils working miracles (Revelation 16;14)

While some of the Scriptures name several spirits such as jealousy, fear and depression and heaviness; there were others that caused sickness. The Bible mentions a spirit that triggers one to believe a lie and a host of unclean and evil spirits. The unclean lead people into all kinds of immorality. From these, we discover that there are hierarchies of angels and demons. We also learn that more than one spirit enters a person, Mary Magdalene had seven (Luke 11:26). mentions a spirit, which once cast out brings seven more along with him to enter the person. There was also the demon who identified itself as Legion because there were many in the person (Mark 5:9, 5:15).

Hierarchy of Demons

Ephesians 6:12 established this hierarchy by stating: *"For we do not wrestle against principalities, against powers, against the rulers of the darkness of this age, against spiritual hosts of wickedness in the heavenly places."*

We know that Lucifer was a fallen angel, most likely an archangel, and he took a third of the angels with him when he fell from grace. The Bible identify several demons who have rank over others. The Scriptures name Michael the Archangel who is over Israel. In contrast to the demonic activity, we also read In Zechariah 6:5 of the four spirits, which go forth from standing before the Lord of all the earth. Revelation 1:4, 3:1, 4:5 and 5:6 also mention the seven Spirits of God before the throne, which God sends into all the earth.

A spiritual battle takes place alongside of our physical earth. Some refer to this as the Battle of the Ages between God and Satan. Satan's aim against humankind is to destroy as many people, to keep them from ever knowing the truth of the Gospel. Satan attempts to keep those who know the Gospel from being effective for Christ.

How does this affect the addict, the Devil wants you dead because if he can kill you, he can keep you from ever being a problem. If he cannot kill you, he wants you in bondage. If you open the door, he will come in and take you. You unlock your door with your heart and deeds.

Along with a spirit of addiction, there are other spirits that come in through trauma. For example at the moment of sexual abuse the victim experiences distress and feels used, controlled, helpless, confused, angry, and worthless. If the victim is not focused on God, a stronghold can attach to the person.

Spirits That Come in That Cause Sex addiction
Spirit of sex addiction
Spirit of pornography
Various unclean spirits driving into various sexual behaviors
Relationship addiction
Love addiction
Seducing spirits
Spirit of abuser to use and abuse others sexually
Spirit of control due to the loss of control
Spirit of hate of men
Spirit of worthlessness
Rejection spirit
Spirit of gluttony (food addiction)
Alcohol addiction
Obsession spirit (wants more and cannot stop)

Suppose it is a male, who his mother verbally and physically abused,

Spirit of alcohol and drug addiction
Spirit of hatred of women
Rejection spirit
Seducing spirits
Spirit of control
Spirit of mistrust
Spirit of his abuser
Lying spirit

Each of the spirits vary depending on the ordeal and what the person experienced during the trauma and what they let in by giving their heart to fill the void left by the damage. The above are only examples of how demonic oppression works.

Trauma comes from many sources: divorce, and physical and or sexual abuse, verbal abuse, living through a natural disaster or war and the list goes on. These spirits become the enemy in our land that we must drive away. Sometimes we can push these foes within our spirit out quickly, and others can take a while and are more stubborn. These spirits are behind our addictions. Total reliance on God drives them out. In addition, you can pray various prayers to help send some of them away. A guide for prayer is as follows:

Return to the trauma
Go back to the original feeling
See what you let in based on that feeling.
Confess any sin and pray the spirit out that you let in. If there are any articles of clothing, memorabilia, or physical objects related to that sin destroy it.

When you uncover one layer, you might not be aware of the one beneath it. Rid yourself of the spirits one at a time. You might have strongholds that are more stubborn to pray off of you, and always pray in the name of Jesus and cover yourself in His blood. As Jesus said, some are so strong they only come out by prayer and fasting.

Succeeding Spiritually And Overcoming the Desire for More

Addicts are preoccupied with their own lives and their vices to make them feel whole or better, although they feel worse after a bender. One of the plagues that comes with addiction is shame. How satisfied we feel as we are indulging in alcohol or drugs, only to feel discrace afterwards. How fulfilled a food addict feels as they overeat and eat foods that are bad for them to experience guilt and defeat afterward. How gratified the sex addict feels when they have another fling until later when they feel used because this is not what they really want.

Addicts consume themselves with themselves, which is why many of them show narcissistic behaviors. The further one is into their idolatry the more preoccupied with self they become. Successful spirituality is the death of self. Only by dying to self- do we truly live. We think that if we take care of ourselves, in other words, have all that we need or desire, we will get better. On the contrary, the more we die to ourselves the larger we live. Matthew 16:24 states, *"Then Jesus said to his disciples, "if anyone desires to come after Me, let him deny himself, and take up his cross and follow me. For whoever desires to save his life will lose it, but whoever loses his life for My sake will find it."*

A military Colonel who received the combat infantry badge fought in battle for an extended length of time. He stated that he survived combat because the minute he went into the fire-fight, he realized that he was dead. He knew that there was no way he was going to survive the battle. In his spirit, he actually died and accepted death. He attributes this mindset to his ability to survive combat.

Many addicts are into the "poor me" syndrome. "Poor me, poor me, pour me another drink." They are obsessed with those who have wronged them and are co-dependent, angry and resentful. It is all about them. Jesus further elaborates on the death to self-principle when he states in Mark 10:27, *"He who loves father or mother more than me is not worthy of me, and he who loves son and daughter more than me is not worthy of me. And he who does not take up his cross and follow after Me is not worthy of Me And he who does not take up his cross and follow after Me is not worthy of Me. He who finds his life will lose it and he who loses his life for My sake will find it."*

If you are a love addict, and you are obsessed with your relationship, you have to leave that person behind and follow Jesus. If you are an addict and anger fuels your vice or resentment against someone, you have to free yourself of that adversary in addition to forgiving them. Sometimes even after we forgive we find ourselves obsessed about the person's deeds, and it is here we must focus on our walk with Christ and our mission for Him. You might ask: what is your mission? Your first mission is to heal your addiction and make a difference in the lives your vice has most likely destroyed or impacted negatively--those of your family.

Know Ye Not Your Body is the Temple

Most addicts completely ignore 1 Corinthians 6:19, which states, *"Or do you not know that your body is the temple of the Holy Spirit who is in you, whom you have from God, and you are not your own? For you were bought at a price, therefore, glorify God in your body and in your spirit which are God's."* This verse comes after Paul's command to flee sexual immorality. For the addict who is all about seeking pleasure this verse is incomprehensible. The addict has taken his or her body as their own. Their body is not a temple of the Holy Spirit but a temple for their drug of choice, which includes sex and food addiction. The addict does not consecrate themselves to God no matter how self-destructive their vice.

In giving their heart to their addiction of choice, their body goes with it as well. The reason an addict cannot give his or her body to God is that they have not given their heart. Where your heart is your legs will follow. Romans 12:1 elaborates, *"I beseech your therefore, brethren, by the mercies of God, that you present your bodies a living sacrifice, holy, acceptable to God, which is your reasonable service."* For the addict, this verse does not mean anything because he or she cannot comprehend their body belonging to anyone, but himself or herself. The addict ignores these words.

Although the addict disregards the verse relating to their body being the temple of God and does not apply it, he or she can aid their deliverance by doing the following:

Take the parts of your body that you used for your sin and your addiction and give them to God. Envision yourself placing them on his altar and next consecrate those parts to God.

Make a sacrifice of the part of your body you sin with and give it to God. If food is your addiction, consecrate your mouth, your stomach and give up a food to Him that normally you would not be able to resist, give it to God as a sacrifice that you make to Him. This goes down the pike to alcohol, drugs, sex, gambling. It sounds crazy to give the parts of your body you sin with or your sin to God as a sacrifice but remember you have made these things gods, and you are now in bondage to them. If you are obsessed with a person, then offer that person up to God as a sacrifice. As you pray to give God the parts of your body that you use for your addiction you will begin to get freedom from your vice. This will help with your deliverance and from your obsession for more.

Ultimately, the desire for more will wane with each day that you stay sober and clean. For substance abuse addictions, the longing to use will creep up out of nowhere. You will be at an event with a wine tasting, and a little voice will tell you to have a sip, that it is okay. You will suddenly get an urge for a cigarette when you have not had a desire for several years. These thoughts get easier to ignore the longer you go without using. The desire will also come up in dreams and sometimes these occur when these thoughts are the furthest from your mind. You will dream that you drank again, drugged or smoked a cigarette. In the nightmare, you feel the horror for having slipped, but wake up relieved that it was after all only a dream. You must be careful and stay away and never indulge again.

I heard the case of a woman who quit smoking for many years. She took one drag of a cigarette, which she did not feel would hurt, and it started her smoking all over again. The same applies to alcohol. The addiction begins with one sip. For the addict, it is all or nothing. There is no in-between.

9

HERBS TO AID RECOVERY

There are herbs, which can help addicts kick the habit to addictive substances, aid them when experiencing withdrawals. They also help the body heal and recover from the damage the drugs caused more quickly. Alcohol and drugs are very hard on one's health. Recovery should not only be about restoring our spiritual strength, but also our physical bodies. A well-nourished body lends to a sound mind. Cleaning out the body and repairing one's health is not only good for the healing process but also for the recovery plan. When you spend the time, money and effort for what it takes to reverse the damage from substance abuse or overeating, you will not want to damage your body again so easily.

Ezekiel 47:12 tells us concerning certain trees that grow along the bank of a river in Israel, *"Their fruit will be for food, and their leaves for medicine."* Plants in their entirety, in the form that God made them have some incredible healing properties. There are herbs that are effective in helping the body withdrawal from various drugs along with detoxing and rebuilding from them. In addition, there are herbs, which can calm an addict without the side effects and dependency that comes with street or pharmaceutical drugs.

This chapter will provide you a good overview on the use of herbs for withdrawal from addictive substances. It also furnishes a list of herbs to help rebuild your body from the damage caused by toxic street drugs.

Before we begin the list of herbs, it should be noted that eating a healthy diet in addition to taking herbs is paramount during recovery. Speaking of diet, one of the reasons for the physical dependency of tobacco, alcohol, chocolate and carbohydrates is that addicts are actually allergic to these substances. When one has a food or drug allergy, the food sensitivity causes one to crave the very foods to which they are hypersensitive. According to the Mayo Clinic, alcohol allergy is exhibited by the body's inability to break it down. Sugar, caffeine, nicotine and alcohol are all highly allergic substances and cravings are a symptom of food allergies. The only way to break the allergy is the stop using the food or drug. In addition, these substances do not behave normally in the body of an addict.

For Cigarette Smoking Cessation

Lobelia contains an alkaloid named lobeline. Lobeline has a molecular structure similar to nicotine. It attaches to the same receptor sites as nicotine and helps to curb the craving for cigarettes. Lobelia is a natural expectorant, thus it is good to use to alleviate lung congestion.

The Indians used Lobelia to treat pneumonia among other respiratory illnesses and infections. Besides helping smokers control their cravings for nicotine, Lobelia also makes cigarettes taste unpleasant. Called Indian tobacco, Lobelia has similar effects on the body as nicotine. Lobelia helps people fight the effects of nicotine withdrawal. Lobelia may increase levels of the neurotransmitter dopamine in the brain similar to cigarettes. Drink it in a tea and up to four cups a day. In addition to Lobelia, you might want to add some other herbs.

Cayenne Pepper desensitizes the respiratory system to tobacco and chemical irritants thereby thwarting the cravings for cigarettes.

Ginseng prevents the nicotine-induced release of the neurotransmitter dopamine and can help alleviate the number of cravings.

St. John's Wort is an herbal antidepressant, and can also help people quit smoking.

For Alcohol Withdrawal

Kudzu: The Chinese have used the traditional Chinese herb Kudzu to reduce alcohol drinking in China since 600 A.D. You can take 3 to 5 g per day of Kudzu root extract within a 24 hour period or 3 to 4 ml of tincture three times daily to reduce alcohol cravings, says the University of Michigan Health System. According to an article written by Associated Press medical researcher Scott Lukas, Kudzu appears to have been discovered to be a compound that is effective in reducing alcohol intake.

The herb Kudzu can cut alcohol consumption in half without any side effects. Kudzu increases blood-alcohol concentration so that people need less alcohol to feel its effects. Research points to the possibility of Kudzu inhibiting the breakdown of an enzyme that breaks down alcohol. This leaves the drinker feeling satisfied for a longer period. There are also other herbs that are helpful when trying to stop abusing alcohol.

Wood Botany reduces alcohol cravings, agitation and irritability and relieves headaches related to withdrawal.

St John's Wort reduces alcohol consumption and is an important herb in any herbal regime for combating addiction.

Schizandra is an adaptogen and tonic that supports adrenal gland health. It is used by the Chinese to treat mental disorders caused by alcoholism, and it also offers protective benefits for liver health.

B Vitamins Are A Must

It is especially important for a recovering alcoholic to take B vitamins when healing their bodies from alcohol abuse. Alcoholics tend to be deficient in B vitamins, and drinking depletes B vitamins in the body even further. Taking 500 mg of each day can help restore vitamin B levels, but possibly also reduce the individual's cravings for alcohol. Some doctors recommend alcoholics ingest a daily dose of at least 100 mg of B-complex vitamins.

Thiamine or B1 is also extremely important because the deficiency is what causes "wet brain" in alcoholics. The first stage of wet brain is reversible with thiamine supplements but the second stage, while it can improve the symptoms of wet brain, it never comes back totally. If you are actively drinking, be sure to take B vitamins and especially thiamine.

For Cocaine Withdrawal

Korean White Ginseng is an adaptogen, which means it helps the body better deal with stress.

Ginseng helps purify the blood of toxins; alkalizes the body, increases endorphins, increases energy and eases cocaine withdrawal.

Lobelia is comprised of Lobeline. According to animal studies published in the Journal of Pharmacology and Experimental Therapeutics in 2000. Lobeline increases dopamine and norepinephrine release while interfering with receptors associated with addiction. Another study in the same journal in 2001 found that Lobeline blocks the behavioral and neurochemical effects of amphetamine drugs. Lobelia is important in the herbal arsenal as an antidepressant and drug-withdrawal aid.

FREE FROM CAPTIVITY

For Opiate Withdrawal

Kratom prevents withdrawal symptoms in an opiate addict, and eliminates cravings. It also has other medicinal purposes. Kratom's primary alkaloids 7-hydroxymitragynine and mitragynine interact with the opioid receptors.

In as early as 1897 Scientists discovered that the leaves and bark of *Mitragyna speciosa or Kratom* treated opium addiction. Mitragynine was the only constituent isolated from Kratom, which possesses morphine-like properties.

New Zealand uses Kratom for methadone dependence detox. Although chemically similar, ibogaine and mitragynine work by different pathways, and have different applications in treatment of drug dependence. Ibogaine treats opiate cravings. Mitragynine gradually weans users off opiates. The presence of opiate drugs increases mitragynine's crossover because it directs binding to where it is needed, automatically regulating the attachment ratio and modulating it towards the delta receptors over a short time. Thus, a person dependent on opiates would stop use of opiates, and the cravings and withdrawal eased by the binding of mitragynine to the delta receptors. In Southern Thailand, heroin users use Kratom to break their dependence and to manage cravings.

In 1999, Pennapa Sapcharoen, director of the National Institute of Thai Traditional Medicine in Bangkok said that Kratom could be prescribed both for opiate dependence and to patients suffering from depression, but stressed that further research is needed.

Bacopa is an herb used in Ayurveda medicine for memory and stress. Bacopa contains saponins called bacosides that appear to affect the brain by enhancing the neurotransmitters acetylcholine and serotonin. These actions in the brain, along with Bacopa's ability to relieve anxiety and depression and other psychological factors, aid in drug withdrawal. An in-vitro study published in the Journal of Ethnopharmacology in 2002 found that Bacopa extract appeared to ease morphine withdrawal symptoms in a guinea-pig, according to the University of Pittsburgh Medical Center.

Passionflower contains constituents such as alkaloids, maltol and gamma-pyrone derivatives that may activate gamma aminobutyric acid or "GABA" receptors and inhibit monoamine oxidase, causing sedative effects, according to the Memorial Sloan-Kettering Cancer Center. These specific calming actions in the body might help in treating withdrawal symptoms associated with opiates and benzodiazepines. A 2001 double-blind clinical trial of men addicted to opiates published in the Journal of Clinical Pharmacy, and Therapeutics found that taking Passionflower along with the medication Clonidine was more effective at treating the emotional and physical symptoms of drug withdrawal than taking clonidine alone.

Lobelia increases dopamine and norepinephrine release, which account for its potential use as an antidepressant and drug-withdrawal aid.

Rosemary, according to a 2003 study in the journal Phytotherapy Research, found that taking Rosemary extract eased morphine withdrawal symptoms in mice.

Velvet Antler possesses anti-narcotic effects relating to morphine. Two studies using mice published in the Journal of Ethno pharmacology in 1999 discovered that taking a water extract of velvet antler had this effect.

For Methamphetamines

L-Phenylalanine
L-Tyrosine Both of these amino acids restore the brain chemicals norepinephrine and dopamine, which are vital for recovering meth addicts. These amino acids can counteract the symptoms of depression, low energy, lack of focus and concentration. The expected behavior changes when restoring

these depleted amino acids are anti-craving, anti-depression, increased energy, improved mental focus.

Calcium and magnesium in high doses, chelated calcium 1500 mg and magnesium 1000 mg as methamphetamine use depletes magnesium. Magnesium deficiency is also a cause of depression and insomnia.

In addition, cocaine, crack, methamphetamine and amphetamine users will want to take:

Hawthorn Berry, which is a Eurasian herb, is highly regarded for its ability to cure early stages of heart diseases. It helps to improve circulation by dilating the coronary arteries and blood vessels to allow blood and oxygen to circulate all over the body without giving much pressure to the heart. It helps dilate blood vessels and lower blood pressure. Cocaine, amphetamines and methamphetamines constrict blood vessels and can cause a sudden heart attack. It is a heart and circulatory system tonic and is important in amphetamine drug users healing regime.

Liver Supports For Substance Abusers

Many substances are especially damaging to the liver. Crystal meth is full of toxic solvents. Cocaine, crack cocaine, alcohol, inhalants, and many other drugs are especially hard on the liver. Weight that gathers around the mid-section is a classic sign of liver problems.

Milk Thistle is the most important herb in your herbal arsenal to support liver function. Milk Thistle seed extract helps reverse liver damage caused by cirrhosis, hepatitis, fatty liver and mushroom poisoning. Milk Thistle is helpful in the support of the liver, and aids the cleansing of toxins and encourages new cell growth.

If you abused alcohol, Milk Thistle is necessary for the liver. If you have alcohol dependency, taking Milk Thistle may help to treat alcohol-induced liver damage or alcoholic liver disease. Milk Thistle can help to improve liver function, says the University Of Maryland Medical Center. Milk Thistle is most beneficial for people with mild alcohol-related liver damage and is less effective for people with severe liver diseases such as cirrhosis. Milk Thistle may regenerate damaged liver cells and prevent harmful toxins from entering the cells, says the University of Michigan Health System.

Herbalists consider Milk Thistle an effective liver tonic. The silymarin in Milk Thistle works to bind the membranes of the cells in the liver, shielding the organ and its cells from toxin attack. Additionally, the Milk Thistle's silymarin stimulates the liver to produce proteins and enzymes faster, thus enabling it to battle the toxins in your body at a quicker rate. Milk Thistle works best taken in combination with food. In addition to helping detoxify the liver of poisons such as alcohol, Milk Thistle stimulates bile production and improves digestion, helps break down fats in foods for optimal cholesterol levels, provides antioxidants to combat the accumulation of free radicals, aids in reducing inflammation of the liver and gallbladder and may help in stress relief.

In addition to Milk Thistle, other herbs, which benefit the liver include:

Dandelion Root is a liver detoxifier that can help repair damage due to alcohol or liver harming prescription drugs. It enhances nutrient absorption.

Burdock eliminates wastes and is a liver and lung tonic. It contains the carbohydrate inulin that strengthens the liver. It is also a detoxifier because it eliminates toxins through the skin.

Bupleurum is an exceptional liver detoxifier. It is widely used in traditional Chinese medicine and is a powerful liver protector even in cases of hepatitis and immune system dysfunction.

Coptis is an herb with known liver-cleansing properties and is especially helpful when it comes to overcoming alcohol addiction. Health-food stores sell it a tincture or in pill form.

Cayenne Pepper comes in ointment, capsule, powder and tincture. Herbalists recommend it primarily for its blood-movement stimulation properties and for removing toxins in the blood. For purposes of ridding your body of toxins related to alcohol and drugs in your addiction fight, take between one and four capsules twice daily, or massage the ointment into the skin once per day.

Turmeric is a natural liver detoxifier, painkiller and anti-inflammatory, and the Chinese use it for depression.

Aloe Vera helps to strengthen the liver.

Schisandra, is a Chinese adaptogen herb, mild sedative and liver protector.

Artichoke aids the liver and has been used as a treatment for hangovers because of its effects on the liver.

N-acetyl cysteine also benefits the liver as an important detoxifier, use 600 mg twice daily.

Fennel aids elimination of toxins, and can be used to treat food poisoning.

In addition to herbs:

Exercise- You should add some form of daily exercise to your routine. Exercise produces endorphins, which are the body's feel good chemicals. Sweating from exercise helps with detoxification.

Saunas and sweating through exercise are among the best ways to remove the body of toxic solvents such as incurred from meth abuse. A twenty-minute sweat followed by a rinse with cold water daily will promote the detoxification of the harsh solvents used in the production of methamphetamines and street drugs.

Epson salt, baking soda baths also detoxify the body. Add one cup of Epson salt and one cup of baking soda and soak for 20 minutes. Epson salt baths contain magnesium and are a good way to get magnesium into your system.

Brushing your body also helps to eliminate toxins and stimulate the lymphatic system.

Removing Heavy Metals Found in Street Drugs

Drug dealers usually cut street drugs with substances containing heavy metals. To help get dangerous metals out of your system add:

Miso Soup contains dipilocolonic acid, which is an alkaloid that can chelate, bind to and remove heavy metals from your body. You can drink miso soup daily to enjoy its health benefits.

Garlic, Cilantro, Burdock Root and **Pectin** found in lemons or apples also remove metals from the body.

Nervous System Support

Nature supplies many herbs, which calm the nervous system and provide additional support for the withdrawal symptoms of coming off substances. It can which take about a year for the body to return to a normalized state. Among the herbs, which are good for the nervous system, are:

Passionflower could help during drug withdrawal, according to the University of Pittsburgh Medical Center. It is a natural relaxer and helps with insomnia.

Rosemary and velvet antler might also have the potential for treating drug withdrawal symptoms.

FREE FROM CAPTIVITY

Catnip calms your mind and helps you relax.

Chamomile eases nervousness; it is good for the liver and lungs, and digestive upsets.

Hops for its calming effect.

Motherwort induces calmness and helps to stabilize emotions.

Skullcap stabilizes mood and is a sedative and tonic. It eases depression, insomnia and restlessness. Scullcap reduces addictions and alcoholism by supporting proper nervous system health and lowering cravings. It is especially helpful for barbiturate addiction and withdrawal. Scullcap has the added benefit of enhancing motor ability and sensory impairment.

St. John's Wort is a mood lifter and aids with withdrawal from various substances and helps prevent viral infections.

Valerian is a natural tranquilizer and a sleep aid that is very effective. It is also a muscle relaxer. Valerian acts as a good sedative and helps relax the central nervous system and decrease levels of anxiety and stress

Albizzia also called the "tree of happiness" is used by Chinese herbalists to ease mild depression, anxiety and stress and as a tonic used in formulas to help overcome addiction.

Oatseed/Oatstraw provides a high source of calcium and magnesium to nourish the nerve sheath. It is calming and grounding especially for addiction with secondary ADHD or hyperactivity.

Ashwagandha is an Ayurvedic nervous system restorative, which can help prevent relapse. It is helpful for "burnout" and withdrawal symptoms like severe daytime fatigue with nighttime insomnia and agitation.

Oatstraw – Helps to rebalance the levels of endorphins.

Yarrow contains a mild hypnotic ingredient called thujone, which has a similar effect to that of marijuana. Yarrow tea is best sipped before bedtime to induce relaxation and deeper, more peaceful sleep. It is used in the therapeutic treatment of inflammation, anxiety, digestive and blood disorders, muscle spasms, wounds, colds, flu, whopping cough and asthma, just to name a few. It is a potent detoxifier that helps improve immune-system health. Yarrow is good for both its relaxation properties, and because it is a detoxifier.

The adaptogen herb's **Licorice, Siberian, Korean Ginseng, Rhodiola** and **Siberian Ginseng** help the body deal with stress and build up the immune system. They also relieve depression.

Brain Tonics For Restoring Brain Chemistry

In addition to the nervous system damage system caused by drugs and alcohol, these substances rearrange brain chemistry. The following brain tonics also provide healing for the addict:

Ginko Biloba a brain tonic rich in vitamin C and niacin.

Butchers Broom increases circulation and blood flow to the brain.

Bacoba improves many brain functions and even helps rejuvenate brain cells.

Superfoods

Alcohol, drugs and tobacco deplete the body of nutrients and cause the body undue stress. Along with using herbs for withdrawal and detox, you will want to add some super foods to your diet to help replenish your body with nutrients and heal your body from the damage of drugs, alcohol and cigarettes.

    If you are not using sea salt and are flavoring with table salt switch to using a good-quality sea salt to obtain minerals your body needs. Eliminate white processed grains for whole grains; eat plenty of fruits, vegetables and lean meat. Eradicate white sugar and satisfy your sweet tooth with only sweets containing organic sugar or pure maple syrup, honey or rice syrup and barley syrup. Stay away from chemical sweeteners like saccharin and aspartame and replace it with packets of stevia, which sells in supermarkets. Stevia is from a plant 300 times sweeter than sugar.

Superfoods that you will want to include in your diet include:

Bee Pollen: enhances adrenal gland functioning and contains five to seven times the amount of protein as beef for blood sugar stabilization. It is nutritionally complete with all 22 amino acids, 27 minerals, vitamins, complex carbohydrates, EFAs, enzymes and co-enzymes.

Kelp/Sea Vegetables provide one of the highest sources of minerals available. It is rich in body building minerals like calcium, iron, iodine and potassium.

Barley Grass is a green grass that can provide sole nutritional support to an animal throughout life. It possesses ten times more calcium than cow's milk and is a good vegetarian source of B12. It also neutralizes heavy metals like mercury.

Alfalfa is a nutritional powerhouse, pulling up minerals from the soil from depths as great as 130 feet.

Nettles are very high mineral source, including potassium, calcium, magnesium and silica.

Goji Berries are the most nutrient-rich food on the planet. With over 15% protein, 21 essential minerals, and 18 amino acids, as well as lycium barbarum polysaccharides (LBP). Goji berry is a nutrient-dense superfood. Here are just a few of the many benefits you get from eating goji berries:

They strengthen the immune system.
Provide antioxidant and anti-aging effects
Protect the liver
Builds strong blood and promotes cardiovascular health.
Supports eye health and improves vision and combat's premature aging.

Goji's have an almost perfect amino acid complex in conjunction with valuable trace minerals, vital to proper muscle contraction and regeneration.

Herbal Benzos For Anxiety

Now that you have all the herbs and foods to help heal and repair your body, there might come a time when life's circumstances become so overwhelming such as during times of grief or loss that you might need an herb with a strong sedative effect. Most addicts suffer from anxiety, depression, and obsessive thinking. Compulsive thoughts can be positive if channeled for productive activities but during times of stress, addicts will tend to obsess on persons or situations, which cause them pain, and their minds will race with these thoughts. After all an addict in part reaches for substances to ease their anxiety and helps to calm them. While many herbs listed above help with anxiety, the following are much more potent in their relaxation ability.

Sceletium has a remarkable ability to treat symptoms of anxiety. Sceletium tortuosum is a South African plant with a long history of use in South Africa. For hundreds of years, the Hottentots of Southern Africa used Sceletium tortuosum as a mood enhancer, relaxant and empathogen. Natives also refer to it as Kanna. Historically, people chewed, smoked or used as snuff Sceletium tortuosum, *which produces euphoria and alertness, which* gently fades into relaxation. Natives used the plant in rural areas in very small doses as a treatment for colic in infants. They also made a tea made from Sceletium to wean alcoholics off liquor.

The mood-elevating action of Sceletium is caused by a number of alkaloids, including mesembrine, mesembrenol and tortuosamine. These interact with the brain's dopamine and serotonin receptors. Mesembrine is a major alkaloid present in Sceletium. Mesembrine is a potent serotonin-uptake inhibitor and acts as a natural antidepresent.

Mesembrine is an alkaloid within Sceletium is a confirmed serotonin (re)-uptake inhibitor, as understood by the US Patent office, which means that it regulates the effects of one of the brain's most important neurotransmitters. In individuals suffering from depression, the neurotransmitter serotonin (also known as 5-hydroxytryptamine) is lacking. Mesembrine slows down the re-uptake process, making it more probable there will be more serotonin in the relevant receptors, greatly increasing the possibility that there will be sufficient levels to set up the signal transfer in all neighboring neurons. Mesembrine permits the brain to function with reduced levels of serotonin, allowing time for natural levels to build up. Meanwhile, herbalists reduce or eliminate the mesembrine dosage.

A number of psychiatrists, psychologists and doctors use tablets and capsules of Sceletium successfully with excellent results for anxiety states and mild to moderate depression. Overall Sceletium elevates mood and decreases anxiety, stress and tension. In intoxicating doses, it can cause euphoria, initially with stimulation and later with sedation. The plant is not hallucinogenic, and documents do not record severe adverse effects and there is no record that it is addictive.

A typical dose is between 50mg and 100mg once or twice day, usually taken after breakfast and after lunch. Less commonly, this is to 100mg two times a day, if necessary. In drug rehabilitation programs, under physicians or psychiatrist's supervision, the dose needed may be as high as 200mg twice a day. The reported side effects are as follows: mild headache, slight nausea, soft stool with no cramping, initial increase in anxiety or irritability an hour after taking, which lasts about an hour, insomnia, corrected by lowering the does or taking the product no later than midday. If sedation occurs reduce the product to a single 50 mg dose at night.

Kava Root Powder

Kava, which means intoxication pepper, is one of the strongest plants next to opiates for its relaxation effects in the body. Close in composition to benzodiazepines, kava provides relaxation similar to taking a strong dose of Valium. Its muscle relaxation is superior to pharmaceutical muscle relaxers. Kava root powder is sold either instant or dried and consumed in a drink, which is how natives drink it on the South Pacific islands. The beverage delivers 125 times more kavalactones than kava sold in tinctures and capsules. Heat destroys Kavalactones at 140 degrees, which makes the hot kava teas ineffective because the main constituents are destroyed at that temperature.

Kava root powder consumed in a drink imparts an incredible relaxation, a slight euphoria and the user never loses mental clarity or the ability to think clearly. Kava intensifies the senses, and increases focus and can greatly help with obsessive-compulsive thinking while also imparting relaxation. Kava is non-addictive.

Effects of kavalactones include mild sedation, a slight numbing of the gums and mouth, and vivid dreams. Kava improves cognitive performance and promotes a cheerful mood. Kava has similar effects to benzodiazepine medications, including muscle relaxant, anesthetic, anticonvulsive and anxiolytic effects. Research currently suggests kavalactones potentiate $GABA_A$ activity, but do not alter levels of dopamine and serotonin in the CNS.

Desmethoxyyangonin, one of the six major kavalactones, is a reversible MAO-B inhibitor and is able to increase dopamine levels in the brain. This finding might correspond to the slightly euphoric action of kava.

Kavain, another kavalactone inhibits the reuptake of noradrenalin at the transporter but not of serotonin. An elevated extracellular noradrenalin level in the brain may account for the reported enhancement of attention and focus. Kava also detoxifies the body, which is why it should never be consumed with alcohol, because alcohol is a toxin and the combination can make one feel sick.

According to Ernest Campbell, MD the kavalactones, comprise 15% of the root. Of the fifteen lactones isolated from Kava Kava, there are six major lactones (kavalactones) known to provide psychoactive activity: kawain, methysticin, demethoxy-yangonin, dihydrokawain, dihydomethysicin, and yangonin. None of these are water soluble. They are dissolvable in alcohol, oil and other fat solvents, including gastric juices. All kavalactones are physiologically active. The fat-soluble kavalactones derived from kava resin convey the main psychoactive activity. Absorption in the gastrointestinal tract is remarkably rapid, so the effects occur almost immediately.

Synthetic Kava does not possess the same soothing qualities of naturally extracted kavalactones from the Kava plant. Correctly, extracted Kava Kava will contain all six kavalactones in high concentrations (25-30%).

The user feels Kava's effects almost immediately. It has a reverse tolerance, which means that you need to drink less to get the same result once the Kava kicks in. Never mix Kava with benzodiazepine drugs because it can intensify or double the effect of them because they are similar in composition.

Kava grows all over the South Pacific islands, including Hawaii. The various South Pacific islands produce different strains of Kava, which vary in color and effect. The most potent plant comes out of the island of Vanuatu, which is the island of Kava's origination. Vanuatu claims to have named about 265 varieties of Kava. When buying Kava root powder you have to be careful who you purchase it from because unscrupulous business persons are adding saw dust to their Kava's. This author prefers Vanuatu Kava from www.instantkavatea.com for their connoisseur grade Kava. It also sells on Amazon under Vanuatu Kava.

Many alcoholics and opiate addicts have been able to get sober using Kava as a methadone type of treatment for their addiction. Unlike methadone, Kava is not addictive and does not have any adverse effects in the body. It is a true sedative, which addicts can truly benefit from using.

Conclusion

This list of herbs for healing serves to help in withdrawal and also to speed healing and balancing the emotions for the addict.

Recovery is about changing your life. Taking the steps to clean and heal your body will move you forward in a new and beneficial direction. It will also give you something to focus on that is positive to help keep you clean and sober.

10
IT'S YOUR CHOICE

It is almost cliché for many who say that Hell is on earth because life is so difficult and painful. According to the Bible, despite all of your life circumstances you can experience a bit of heaven on earth via the Promised Land. It is a place of joy, happiness and peace and does not compare to anything this world has to offer can offer. You can have it in your life, and I know because I have experienced it.

The Bible says that the fruit of the spirit is love, joy and peace. When we follow God and do all that He asks and yield to the Spirit it fills us. At Pentecost when the Spirit first came upon the disciples, it appeared as tongues of fire. The reason it looked like fire is because fire spreads. When people saw what the disciples possessed, they wanted it. People who are on fire with the Holy Spirit are contagious and others want what they have. Who does not want love, joy and peace in his or her life?

While writing this, I received a phone call from my son, whose drinking was so bad that I sent him down with his father to live, who was also drinking. It was 8:15 in the morning, and my son was crying. His father was so drunk that he stumbled and fell through his glass coffee table. Glass shattered everywhere, and a big piece of glass cut him below his knee. While his father is bleeding profusely, my son tied a tourniquet around his upper leg. Meantime, his dad is yelling, "get me a cigarette." My son calls 911, and an ambulance takes his father to the emergency room. He nearly cut a major artery; they wheeled him into surgery.

My son then related the most horrific details of his time with his dad. He told me that his father would walk around the house yelling. He would not allow our son to sleep, but would start screaming at him, which progressed to his biting him; my son had bite marks up and down his arm. My son had to get away from his father, so he returned home within three weeks of calling me. On his arrival, I noticed a finger-sized hole in his neck. His dad caused this as he went to strangle our son. When I confronted his father, to my surprise, he did not deny this, but stated his frustration at my son's drinking and actions under the influence.

My son reported that his dad was drinking from daybreak until he fell asleep and would be dead shortly due to his continuous drinking. I got on the phone with his family members to see if there was anything anyone could do and all that we could do was pray. Intercessory prayer is a powerful weapon in the battle against addiction. When the Israelites sinned by making a golden calf in the wilderness, God wanted to destroy them in his anger. Exodus 32: 9-14 records how Moses prayed for them and reasoned with God. Moses commented that the Egyptians would say that God brought out His people to destroy them. He actually told God to turn from his fierce wrath. He reminded God of His promise to Abraham, Isaac and Israel that He would multiply their descendants. Exodus 32:14 records God's answer to Moses' prayer; it states, *"So the Lord relented from the harm which He said He would do to His people."*

If you are struggling with addiction, you can ask people to pray for you. There are 800 prayer lines. The 700 Club has one, and you can phone and request prayer any hour of the day. If you love an addicted person, pray for them just as Moses interceded for the Israelites.

After much discussion with Paul's family members, they concluded that they could do nothing to help him. I also could not aid him. He was in God's hands. My mother had lung cancer and was at the end of her life, so I could not leave and go out of State if it were the solution. My mother died, and Paul learned of her death and contacted me. While intoxicated he managed to get a plane ticket, take two flights across country, and get himself in a van to come and meet me. God now placed him directly in my hands. Not only was he there as a comfort to me, but I could now help him.

For my mother's funeral, Paul came up from Florida to attend. I did not see him in a year and five months. He had been drinking continuously. When he arrived, his appearance shocked me. He did not even resemble the same person of one-and-a-half years earlier, and his looks had deteriorated then. He literally looked like he stepped out of the Bowery in New York City, out from underneath a garbage pail. His hair grew to nearly his shoulders and on a middle-aged man with weight, it looked horrible. He wore an orange shirt with a hole in it. The lines were so deep under his eyes; they disfigured his once handsome face.

In him was a spirit of apathy. The spirit kept him in a perpetual state of not caring; there was also a spirit of depression. I prayed these spirits off him, including the spirit of alcohol addiction. During the funeral and the days after he detoxed and he was surprised he made it to the funeral traveling half way across the country in the condition he was in. Although without alcohol his personality had changed, he was angrier and distant.

This occurred in part because of alcohol's effect on the brain. I told him that he needed to take Thiamine and B vitamins to help restore his emotions. He was suffering horrific anxiety, also classic of withdrawal. In part, he had worshiped the god of his vice and given himself over to those demons so many times that he invited many more into his person. Despite this, he began working on his relationship with God and reading the Bible. I verbally instructed him with the teachings in my book. The hardest part for me was dealing with who he became.

I recited to him all that I wrote in this book that I discovered while he detoxed. He also saw a big change in me. He refused to go to a detox center. For five days, he had the shakes, and he took his prescription of Ativan and Xanax to help him with his trembling. During the first few days, he cried out in his sleep, yelling and having conversations with people who were not there.

Paul was a seasoned AA person, who had been in rehabs during his first round of sobriety. I discussed with him the anatomy of an addict and the pleasure button. From there I talked to him about the dangerous substances, and the illusion of his high and alcohol mimics a stroke in the body. I told him about the prison house, that addiction is idolatry. I informed him about herbs and vitamins that will help him through the process. I also prayed for him, prayed addiction, depression and other spirits off him. I educated him on his addiction from how God sees it. He started to follow these principals and also draw closer to God and stay sober. He no longer had a desire to drink. I warned him that he must break down his altars, which included Florida and his mother's beach house in Connecticut because these were the places he drank. He was going to return to Florida and make arrangements to move back to Connecticut.

On the way to the airport our teenage daughter cried the most heartbreaking pleas and sobs and begged him, "Daddy, please don't go." It broke my heart to listen. She cried from the pain in her soul because of all the times he left and never came back. She did not want him to leave for fear that he would not return. I assured her that he was coming back this time.

An addict can find freedom and deliverance from any vice and any sin. Jesus is that powerful. In the Old Testament when persons committed certain sins, the leaders put them to death. Sin is like a cancer that consumes and destroys a person. Once an individual gives himself or herself over to a sin, it overtakes them. Think of greedy persons you know who cannot ever have enough; sexual deviants who are deemed incurable. This is true if they are without Jesus Christ, but Jesus is all-powerful and can deliver the incurable. If he can deliver those from the power of addiction and the devil, he can deliver you, but you must take the right steps.

When Paul went back to Florida, he deviated from his plan and began to make excuses, and I knew this meant possible trouble. I told him that I would speak to him again when he returned to Connecticut because our discussions were turning into a game. I do not believe he was happy with our not talking, but he phoned our daughter. He informed her that he would be up to see her because he was returning shortly. He said some statements that upset her.

I telephoned Paul and confronted him with what he voiced to our daughter. He said that he told her he would like to come back right away, but he is not ready. He denied the statements, he made to her.

A little over, a month after Paul left us; he phoned our daughter from a Connecticut phone number and asked her to call him back. She did not call because she did not want a similar conversation as her last one. We knew her dad was back in Connecticut but instead of returning for his family and to a sober path, he went back at his mother's beach house with his sister who regularly drinks alcohol. I warned him about returning to the cottage--his drinking haunt. For the following month, we suffered one more month of the pain of being second, but this time, he was close by, which made it more difficult. I learned he resumed drinking. I cried out to God and prayed for him daily.

During prayer, a small voice said to me, "he will not hurt you anymore." I thought: God, you are not going to take his life? I felt that good things were ahead. Within days, Paul called me. I had not been talking to him, but he called from his brother John's phone. He was very drunk. Paul told me that he and his sister had a big falling out, and he was at John's house and they were with another man named Danny. Both of these men drank and used heroin and other drugs. Paul stayed away from John in part because of his heroin use, and now he joined him. He and John did not speak for many years, but they made amends and were drinking together.

I said to Paul, "I thought you were not coming back to Connecticut, why did you lie to me?"

Paul replied, "We were fighting."

We chatted a bit, and he elaborated on his argument with his sister, and mentioned wanting to come back to his family. He told me that he started using alcohol practically as soon as he returned to Connecticut. I warned him about going to his mother's beach house. He managed to stay sober in Florida when he left me, but once he returned to his old drinking haunt, he resumed drinking.

Now that Paul was in Connecticut, I expected him to knock at the door or phone me again soon. John and Danny were junkies. I thought that Paul would not want to stay with them for very long for this reason. I was surprised Paul ended up at his brother's. When he fought with his sister, John invited Paul to come to stay with him and provided him a ride. I assumed that with all of them drinking the honeymoon phase of their reunion would end. When Paul drank he became loud, talkative, argumentative and obnoxious.

A week later I awoke and my call log showed a voicemail from John's phone from which Paul had called me. The call came in very around 3:30 a.m. in the morning--a time typical of Paul to telephone me. I figured he wanted to come to me and the kids and leave his brother's house. I listened to the message, and it was John. In a panic, he said, "Erika, Paul is unresponsive. He won't wake up. We can't wake him. The ambulance is here, call me right away."

I phoned John back at 7 a.m. There was no answer. I felt that this was a good sign. They must have revived Paul. He was not answering because he was at the hospital. I had been up late the night before and took a nap. I awoke and noticed about five calls from my son. I saw a car pull up, and my son came to the door. As soon as he came in he told me that Dad died.

From the onset of this book, I hoped that its ending would have included Paul's freedom from captivity and our reuniting as a family. I wanted the happy conclusion. Sadly, Paul's bottom, like Samson's, was death. I watched God work in his life to draw him back to Him. Paul believed in Jesus Christ as his personal Savior. I saw the plagues that came with his idolatry, the blessings withdrawn and God allowing hardships in his life to help direct him back to a sober life. Nothing could stop Paul from drinking and drugging.

FREE FROM CAPTIVITY

Prior to his death, Paul had just drank for 22 days straight about 20-30 beers a day and hardly ate. Several days before he died; he made complaints that could have indicated potential health problems from drinking. I assumed alcohol caused Paul's death but did not know for sure. We waited on an autopsy.

Paul was drinking with his brother John and Danny the day he died. He stole a bottle of hard liquor and swigged it along with his beer. He sat in a chair at the kitchen table and slept with his head in his arms, snoring very loudly. Alcohol relaxes the throat muscles, causing loud snoring. His forehead and the back of his neck sweated profusely. His breathing went shallow. John went to help move him, and his limbs were ice cold. He lifted his head and his lips looked blue, his skin grey in color. His breathing was now shallow as he let out his last breaths. They tried to revive Paul by attempting CPR, could not and called 911. The emergency workers took seven minutes to arrive. The Paramedics worked on Paul for some time and brought him to the hospital, where he died at approximately 4:25 a.m. in the morning.

I was told by Danny that Paul died happy, drinking, having a good time and stealing. Paul was really pleased about the bottle of liquor he had stolen. This is the end of the man who once would only listen to Christian radio, made six figures, was a devoted family man and served in his church by offering his skills. John joked that he lied so much he was holding him accountable for every word he said. He boasted that he almost got him to the point that he no longer lied.

While Paul's death brought great sadness and shock, it also ushered in relief to know his whereabouts at all times. While it is a reprieve to experience the freedom from the hope of his return, at his death a big part of me and my children's world exited. My daughter described it as feeling as if she lost half of herself. The other part of her comes from me. However, because of the hardship Paul put me through; I am closer to God than ever in my life. His death has driven me nearer to my Lord than any time before.

My children are now fatherless. My 16-year-old daughter felt abandoned by her dad. Now he deserted her completely. We knew his death was brought on by alcohol. All of our daughter's future milestones and achievements she will now accomplish without a father to cheer her on. Her dad will not be there to behold his grandchildren when they are born. His children will not share the joy of those births with him. He will not be at their weddings, and I will now attend them alone. More so, with the death of my mother only three months earlier, I expected to lose her and have Paul by my side. I anticipated growing old with Paul and having him to comfort me after my mother's passing. Instead, I am mourning his loss as well.

Paul told me at my mother's funeral that he wished he had died instead of her. He also expressed this wish to my sister. In one of our recent conversations Paul said that he couldn't wait for the day he was with Jesus and was in a sinless body. Paul knew Jesus as his personal Savior. His death reminds me of the parable of the wicked servant in Luke 12:43-48 who felt his master delayed coming and began to drink and beat his servants. His master came for him when he was not expecting him. I would not want to meet my Savior in the evil state Paul lived on the last day of his life. While he is free from his sinful body and his addictions, he will be accountable for his actions. He will not hold the place he could have, had he loved the Lord thy God with all of his heart and had forsaken his idols.

Few people attended his memorial. He cut ties with the friends who would have gone. He gravitated to other addicts who did not care whether he lived or died. Of course, they were not there. He died without a legacy. Our daughter did not go because of his manner of death and the pain this brought her. She felt that she would regress emotionally.

My cousin called me up and told me that he could laminate the printout from the church for the kids. I said maybe for my son, but our daughter would not want it. My son was older; his dad did not begin drinking until he was 16. Our daughter was seven-and-a-half. Afterward, he was only physically in her life for three years. In eight-and-a-half years, he was with us for a little over three of those years. The final year Paul participated in her life was in her 11th year. The last time he lived with us, he returned for five months.

During that period, I finished my book, *"The Seat of the Antichrist: Bible Prophecy and The European Union."* I thought Paul was with us to stay and never would return to using alcohol again. When he left it caused an avalanche of events in my life. It affected each family member and also caused us other hardships. My son's alcoholism surfaced, and my daughter embarked on a dangerous path. I considered this a Satanic attack. In the process of all of this turmoil, I started this book and began to see God's purpose. Rather should I say that this is not what God intended, but he can turn lemons into lemonade. I had no idea that the ending would be this tragic.

I can still see Paul's 94-year-old mother, who I thought for certain would die before him, crying, "my boy, my boy, he was my baby boy." He was the youngest of her six children. She had him late in life. Along with his mom, he left the rest of his family and few friends saddened by his loss.

While Paul's death brings great sadness, in a sense he died a long time ago. He was 23 years sober when he picked up a drink and started using drugs. I knew that it would be life and death for him if he ever drank again. Eight-and-a-half years since after took his first sip and started his downward spiral, he ended up dead.

When Paul started to drink, dealing with him became like dealing directly with the Devil. This once decent man committed actions that were pure evil, against himself, others and his family.

He is now never coming back. Our hope died with his death. My daughter wrote, "the dream is dead." With his end came our release from the pain he caused and our freedom from a hope that would at no time occur. He never completed in his life what God meant for him to accomplish. Like Samson, his bottom was death. Samson defeated more enemies in his death than he did in his life. My feeling is that if Paul were alive and would have known his outcome, he would want me to write every detail as I have done. I will carry his torch and maybe now by his death he will indirectly do more good than he achieved during his life.

Living with an addict, I could relate to 2 Timothy, which speaks about man's wickedness just prior to the Tribulation. I thought that this was occurring in my life so that I could experience what I was writing about concerning the difficulties of living in these Last Days.

The prophets of God as writers and teachers suffered many difficulties. They often lived the message God wanted to relay. God commanded Hosea to marry a prostitute and have children with her and told Hosea she would be unfaithful to him. She left Hosea for another man. Hosea prayed for her. Her lover ended up deserting her and selling her naked as a slave. Hosea went to the auction and outbid everyone else to get her back. He told her that she would no longer be a harlot and would be his wife for the rest of her life. God used Hosea's life as a picture of His love for us. Many times we stray from Him for those things we love more than Him.

I think of Ezekiel, whose wife died suddenly and God used her death, as an illustration, for His message. God also made Ezekiel become mute so that the only words he could speak were, "Thus says the Lord." He warned Ezekiel that he will find himself bound in the same way Jesus foretold to Peter. God also paralyzed his side to drive home another message to the Israelites. He lay on his side around a model of Israel and a depiction of what was coming from God if they did not repent. The prophets were forced to live their messages.

I am now living this message. My mother, who I lost three months ago, was also a believer. Unlike Paul, she had a glorious exit. I wrote about it in an article, which is published on Yahoo titled, "What Happens When A Christian Dies." I believe Paul would have had lived a longer life if he did not choose his destructive path.

Paul's life should come to you as a warning. Do not let what happened in his life, befall you. You might wonder why I am not angry at God. I watched God work in his life and try to draw him to Himself over and over. If I learned an even greater lesson, it is the importance of our relationship with the Lord of Hosts. He must be first in our lives.

Paul's official cause of death was respiratory failure. It was brought on by an alcohol level that was three times over the limit, the muscle relaxer Soma that he took for pain in his arms, and shockingly heroin. In our conversations, John hinted that they might find heroin in the autopsy because Paul was asking Danny a lot of questions about using the drug. In his first story he said Paul inquired that day. In a second tale, the asking took place a week earlier. He advised me that Paul would have gotten heroin on his own and they did not give it to him.

Immediately after the autopsy came out, John informed me that he gave a half a bag of heroin to Paul earlier in the day because he demanded it. This changed from his telling me that Paul did not take any drugs that he knew of. He claimed that when Paul inquired about heroin he asked Danny and would not ask him because he had always put John down for using heroin. Now Paul demanded heroin from him, and John gave it to him. John claimed he fell asleep early in the night at 10.p.m., and Paul was awake with Danny who must have given him the heroin. John said he learned the day after that Danny gave Paul two bags earlier on the day he died.

John now blamed his friend for Paul's death. He told me Danny never liked Paul and he knew better than to give Paul so much heroin and that Danny was evil. I discovered later that John did not want his family knowing that Paul used heroin with him because they would have blamed him for Paul's death or held him responsible. The truth was that Paul started to use heroin that week with John and Danny along with cocaine, Xanax and Soma in addition to alcohol. Another addict who was with them told me that Paul "was up for anything" and "he would have done rat poison" if you gave it to him.

Paul lied about his addiction. He especially hid his drug use from his family. Numbers 32:23 states that *"your sin will find you out."* Jesus said in Luke 8:17, *"For nothing is secret that will not be revealed..."* At Paul's death, his body revealed the secrets of his drug use he tried to hide.

Sadly, both John and Danny ransacked Paul's belongings and took anything they could use. They went through his wallet, medicines, and even tried on his eye glasses to see if they could wear them. When they called the EMTs and stated that Paul was unresponsive there was no mention of heroin. The treatment for a heroin overdose might have saved his life. Making such an admission would have revealed their use of an illegal drug. I was told by another addict that in the circles he ran in New York City, they threw those who overdosed out the window because they wanted to protect themselves and not get in any trouble for using illicit drugs.

Paul should not have died that day. He did have underlying serious health conditions, in part brought on by his lifestyle, but this did not kill him. Paul did not have to go to his brothers to stay; he had other places he could have gone. His original plan was to remain sober and reunite with his family. He could have showed up on my doorstep.

In the end, it was Paul's choice. Instead of electing his family, he chose to drink and drug with junkies. Sadly not one of Paul's family members was with Paul when he died. John refused to go into the room and see Paul when he learned of his death. He did not notify anyone until Paul's body was removed. Paul died alone. Paul developed health problems when he lived in Florida. He ended up in the hospital about three times. The kids and I could not be with him because he lived in Florida when these illnesses occurred. Paul abandoned us for his addiction, and himself ended up alone during his life's greatest difficulties, including his passing.

Having gone through all of what I have experienced and most recently Paul's death, which is difficult beyond what you can imagine, I will not go back to any of my vices, not chain cigarette smoking, which I did for 20 years, or alcohol or drugs. This is not to say the temptations have not come into my mind, because they have.

I am no different than Paul; if I pick up, it will be life and death for me too. If I can do it, you can do it. Nearly three months after Paul's death, his sister who was my good friend passed away from cancer. In six months' time I experienced three deaths and the world that I knew changed forever. Despite the extreme pain of these life events, I will not go back to alcohol or drugs. Instead, I will continue to rely on the Lord my God and thank Him for all He is doing in my life. You see I left the prison house and today am as the apostle Paul a bondservant for the Lord Jesus Christ. In being His slave, I am totally free.

John phoned me and told me that he was drinking excessively since Paul's passing and he was afraid he was going to die in his sleep like Paul. He went to a rehab for two days, came out and resumed drinking and drugging. I warned him that he could be next. John insisted that he was not going to die. Sadly, four months after Paul's death and only seven weeks after his sister's passing, John died exactly as Paul after drinking alcohol and shooting heroin. He passed away while sitting as a passenger in the front seat of a car. Ironically, Paul prided that his addiction was not as bad as John's. Yet, they died identical deaths using the same drugs four months apart. In this short time, their 94 year old mother lost three of her five remaining children.

You have to know how I loved Paul. I never wanted to let him go. He was the delight to my eyes. I loved just gazing at him. At times, I would look at him and think he was the most beautiful man, I could ever lay my eyes on. He looked perfect to me. When I held him, it was like holding my own flesh and just hearing his voice made me happy. When he was next to me, I felt content. We had a chemistry that was so powerful I do not think it is humanly capable for me ever experience that again. My hope, and I am sure Paul's hope, would be that you will heed the message in this book and save your life, unlike Paul was unable to save his. He had the information within these pages. He could have had the victory, but he chose not to. In the end, God left the choice to him as He also leaves it to you.

BIBLIOGRAPHY

Chapter 2

Cannabis: What is Cannabis, What are its Effects? Mental Health Foundation of New Zealand, everybody.co.nz June 2005, http://www.everybody.co.nz/page-853942d3-9e56-4a67-b02b-64622fb9abed.aspx

The International Drug Evaluation and Classification Program, www.decp.org, The 7 Drug Categories, n.d., http://www.decp.org/experts/7categories.htm

World Health Report 2002 Reducing Risks Promoting Healthy Life, World Health Organization

Global Status Report on Alcohol and Health 2004 and 2011 World Health Organization

Markus Becker, "International Cocaine Consumption: New York Blows Away The Competition" http://www.spiegel.de/international/international-cocaine-consumption-new-york-blows-away-the-competition-a-450078.html

D.B. Ryan, "How Opiates Work," Livestrong, October 28, 2009, http://www.livestrong.com/article/30370-opiates work/#ixzz1qRtEnoV3

Chris Sherwood, How Do Opiates Work? eHow ,How Do Opiates Work? n.d., eHow.com http://www.ehow.com/how-does_4926987_opiates-work.html#ixzz1qRBv8B00

By Mary Wisniewski RPT-Painkiller Opana, new scourge of rural America, Reuters, March 27,2012,
http://www.reuters.com/article/2012/03/27/drugs-abuse-opana-idUSL2E8EQJOQ20120327

The New York Times, August 31, 2012OxyContin (Drug), http://topics.nytimes.com/top/news/health/diseasesconditions andhealthtopics/oxycontindrug/index.html

Maxim W. Furek, MA, CAC, The Silent Killer: Inhalant Abuse jungle@epix.nethttp://www.fullspectrumrecovery.com/fullspec /images/stories/pdfs/Inhalant%20.pdf

The United States Department of Justice, National Drug Intelligence Center , n.d.,
http://www.justice.gov/ndic/pubs4/4440/index.htm

Chapter 3

David Zieve, MD, MHA, Rush University Medical Center, 6/24/2011,
http://health.rush.edu/healthinformation/hie%20multimedia/1 /000726.aspx

Jerry Kennard, The Physical Effects of Alcoholism, About.com, n.d.June 8, 2006,
http://menshealth.about.com/od/diseases/a/alcohol.htm

Jeff Herten, MD, The Sobering Truth Sobering Truth Press, August 2010,
http://www.soberingtruth.com/index.php/single/chapter_3

Jack G. Modell, Protracted Benzodiazepine Withdrawal Syndrome: Mimicking Psychotic Depression,
M.D.Psychosomatics · Volume 38 · Number 2 · March-April 1997 http://www.bcnc.org.uk/howtheywork.htm

Some Things You Should Know About Cocaine, National Council on Alcoholism and Drug Abuse St. Louis Area, July 09, http://www.ncadastl.org/factsheets/some_things_you_should_know_about_cocaine.pdf

Inhalant Abuse Prevention, Inhalant Abuse, n.d. http://www.inhalant.org/inhalant/dangers.php

United States Department of Justice, National Drug Abuse Intelligence Center, n.d.
http://www.justice.gov/ndic/pubs4/4440/index.htm#Who%20uses

Alcohol and Mental Illness Laurence M. Westreich, M.D., January 2005, http://mbldownloads.com/0105PP_Westreich.pdf

Chapter 4

The Unedited Full Text of the 1906 Jewish Encyclopedia, Molech, Moloch, n.d.
http://www.jewishencyclopedia.com/articles/10937-moloch-molech

David J. Stewart, Bohemian Grove and Molech Worship Jesusissavior.com, http://www.jesus-is-savior.com/ False%20Religions/Wicca%20&%20Witchcraft/bohemian_moloch.htm

Chapter 5

Wayne Blank, Sackcloth and Ashes, The Church of God Daily Bible Study, n.d.
http://www.keyway.ca/htm2002/20020421.htm

Chapter 9

Sarah Terry, Herbal Remedy to Overcome Drug Withdrawal, LiveStrong, July 6, 2010, http://www.livestrong.com/article/167140-herbal-remedy-to-overcome-drug-withdrawal/

William Jackson, Alcoholism and Addiction Cures, n.d., eHow Contributor, eHow.com http://www.ehow.com/way_5368715_alchoholism-addiction-cures.html#ixzz25BCn8Cidhttp://methdrugaddiction.com/72791/help-drug-addicts-with-the-use-of-herbs/Alchoholism and Addiction Cures | eHow.com http://www.ehow.com/way_5368715_alchoholism-addiction-cures.html#ixzz1uPfROMU1

Natural anxiety remedies that really make a difference, Calm Clinic Natural & Herbal Anxiety Remedies calmclinic.com,n.d.,http://www.calmclinic.com/anxiety/natural-herbal-remedies

Sarah Terry, Herbs for Alcohol Dependency LiveStrong, May 23, 2010 http://www.livestrong.com/article/129561-herbs-alcohol-dependency/#ixzz1tvNUw5ae

Alena Bowers, How to Use Lobelia to Quit Smoking LiveStrong, Aug 3, 2010 http://www.livestrong.com/article/192194-how-to-use-lobelia-to-quit-smoking/#ixzz25BEWaM7D

Annie B. Bond, Herbs to Help Stop Smoking Care2, November 18, 2009, http://www.care2.com/greenliving/herbs-to-help-stop-smoking.html#ixzz25BEwwtIs

Benefits of Organic Milk Thistle, Global Healing Center, n.d. http://www.globalhealingcenter.com/benefits-of/organic-milk-thistle-seed

Chester Ku-Lea Ginseng and Its Many Uses, Health Guidance, n.d., http://www.healthguidance.org/entry/3447/1/Ginseng-and-Its-Many-Uses.html

Dr. Nicole Sundene, Natural Healing from Drug Abuse: Meth Amphetamines, Kitchen Table Medicine, June 18, 2008, http://www.kitchentablemedicine.com/natural-healing-from-meth-addiction-and-drug-abuse/

Jordan A Miller Co-Author: Kyla Miller, Natural Remedies to Help You Quit Smoking, Ezine Articles, n.d.,http://ezinearticles.com/?Natural-Remedies-to-Help-You-Quit-Smoking&id=6952123

Dr. Linda Page, Overcoming Addiction With Whole Herbs, Healthier Talk, May 7, 2009, n.d., http://www.healthiertalk.com/overcoming-addictions-whole-herbs-0565

Howard Jamison, Overcome Addictions With Herbal Remedies, Overcoming Addictions Alternative Health Guide, Addictionsolutionsource , n.d. http://www.addictionsolutionsource.com/drug_addiction_treatment/overcome-addictions-with-herbal-remedies

Mayo Clinic Staff, Alcohol Intolerance, Mayo Clinic, April 26, 2012, http://www.mayoclinic.com/health/alcohol-intolerance/ds01172

20 Health Benefits of Turmeric, Eat This! Health Diaries October 1, 2007, http://www.healthdiaries.com/eatthis/20-health-benefits-of-turmeric.html

Turmeric Benefits and Side Effects, The Herbal Resource, n.d., http://www.herbal-supplement-resource.com/turmeric-benefits.html

Cathy Wong, Bacapa: What You need to know about Bacopa, About.Com March 1, 2012, http://altmedicine.about.com/od/completeazindex/a/benefits_bacopa.htm

What is Wet Brain? Hams Harm Reduction Network, 2009, http://hamsnetwork.org/wetbrain/

kanna sceletium tortuosum, neurosoup, n.d., http://www.neurosoup.com/kanna.htm

8 Health Benefits of Artichokes, Eat This! Health Diaries, November 10,2010, http://www.healthdiaries.com/eatthis/8-health-benefits-of-artichokes.html

Sara Janis, Epson Salts for Detox, EHow, n.d., http://www.ehow.com/way_5557410_epsom-salts-detox.html

Lindsay Staker, Foods To Cleanse Heavy Metals, LiveStrong, July 14, 2010 http://www.livestrong.com/article/174503-foods-to-cleanse-heavy-metals/

The Soothing Health Benefits of Yarrow Tea, Health on a Budget, January 19, 2012, http://healthonabudget.com/the-soothing-health-benefits-of-yarrow-tea/

Marilyn Light, Burdock: The Benefits of the Use of Burdock In Herbal Preparations, n.d., http://www.herballegacy.com/Light_Medicinal.html

Dr. Shiroma, Goji Berry-Number 1 Superfood Goji Berries Health Benefits, n.d., http://www.gojiberrieshealthbenefits.com/

www.ingramcontent.com/pod-product-compliance
Lightning Source LLC
Chambersburg PA
CBHW070547170426
43201CB00012B/1753